Multiband Non-Invasive Microwave Sensor

Design and Analysis

Multiband Non-Invasive Microwave Sensor

Design and Analysis

Brijesh Iyer
Nagendra Prasad Pathak

CRC Press
Taylor & Francis Group
Boca Raton London New York

CRC Press is an imprint of the
Taylor & Francis Group, an **informa** business

CRC Press
Taylor & Francis Group
6000 Broken Sound Parkway NW, Suite 300
Boca Raton, FL 33487-2742

First issued in paperback 2020

ISBN-13: 978-0-367-57171-9 (pbk)
ISBN-13: 978-1-138-30098-9 (hbk)

Library of Congress Cataloging-in-Publication Data

Names: Iyer, Brijesh, author. | Pathak, Nagendra Prasad, author.
Title: Multiband non-invasive microwave sensor : design and analysis / Brijesh Iyer, Nagendra Prasad Pathak.
Description: First edition. | Boca Raton, FL : CRC Press, Taylor & Francis Group, 2018. | Includes bibliographical references and index.
Identifiers: LCCN 2017049171| ISBN 9781138300989 (hardback : acid-free paper) | ISBN 9780203732946 (ebook)
Subjects: LCSH: Biosensors--Design and construction. | Search and rescue operations--Equipment and supplies. | Vital signs. | Bioelectronics. | Microwave antennas--Design and construction.
Classification: LCC R857.B54 I94 2018 | DDC 610.28--dc23
LC record available at https://lccn.loc.gov/2017049171

Visit the Taylor & Francis Web site at
http://www.taylorandfrancis.com

and the CRC Press Web site at
http://www.crcpress.com

ईशवराचा लेश मिळे तरि ।

मूढ यत्न शेवटि जातो ।।

With a smallest measure of God's grace ....

Even the mediocre attempt comes to fruition.

Contents

Preface

Conventionally, human vital signs are detected using invasive methods. Non-invasive detection of vital signs is an attractive alternative to conventional methods the due to its two-fold advantage. First, attention and cooperation of the human subject under test are optional. Secondly, it does not cause distress to the human being as in the case of conventional methods. In addition, the non-invasive method of human vital sign detection is, in general, free from periodic maintenance.

Since the 1970s, researchers and academicians started the effort toward the development of RF systems based on the Doppler principle for applications including healthcare, military, and disaster management. All such reported efforts are characterized by their non-invasiveness and use of a particular single band during measurements.

A number of noteworthy research groups, such as the Centre for Radio Frequency Electronics Research (CREER) in Canada; the Radio Frequency Circuits and Systems (RFCS) research group at the University of Florida; the Department of Electrical Engineering at the University of Hawaii; Yonsei University in Seoul, Korea; the WiPLi Lab in the University of Udine, Italy; and the University of Illinois in Chicago, carried out research toward the development of a human VSD radar. In India, research groups at several premier technological institutes, such as the Centre for Applied Research in Electronics (CARE), IIT Delhi, IIT Kanpur, IISc Bangalore, and IIT Roorkee, are engaged in the design and development of non-invasive RF sensors for a variety of day-to-day applications. IIT Bombay in Mumbai is also engaged in the study of the biological effects of radiation on the human body.

For any non-invasive human vital sign measurement system, detection accuracy and sensitivity are two very crucial factors. With single-band operation, either accuracy or noise sensitivity in detection can be achieved in a particular operation. The challenging issue ahead of the existing single-band non-invasive vital sign detection (NIVSD) system is to bridge the trade-off between detection sensitivity and the amount of noise in the received signal. The performance of the existing single-band NIVSD systems may be improved by using multiband operation. While higher frequency allows signal detection even with very minute variations but at the cost of increased noise, the lower frequency band minimizes noise with inferior detection sensitivity. The cross-correlation between the individual baseband signals will emphasize significant information present in both the bands while suppressing unwanted signal components.

A concurrent multiband system can fulfill these requirements. Multiband transceiver architecture may be devised using parallel, switchable, or concurrent arrangements of basic functional blocks. Use of parallel system architecture for the concurrent operation is less attractive due to high power consumption, complex hardware, and its bulky nature. A switched mode multiband system suffers from the drawback of inconsistent measurement conditions for the same human subject due to switching delay. Consequently, these two schemes are not viable due to one or more reasons, such as the requirement of large hardware, high power consumption, or complex radio architecture.

The current trend in the area of microwave-/millimeter-wave integrated circuit research is to reduce the system losses, component count, and power consumption levels so that the RF systems can be used as a portable hand-held device. A concurrent multiband system, based on hardware sharing, fulfills all of these criteria. In view of this, the book aims to review and discuss the design, implementation, and characterization of a concurrent dual-band RF sensor for the non-invasive detection of human vital signs.

Despite many vital signs, human life and its existence can be best ascertained by virtue of its respiration and heartbeat signal. Hence, respiration and heartbeat signal are used as vital signs for this experimentation.

The proposed sensor operates simultaneously at dual frequency bands centered at 2.44 GHz and 5.25 GHz. The sensor prototype is developed using indigenously designed concurrent dual band subsystems and few commercially available components. Finally, a hardware prototype of the proposed RF sensor has been developed and experimentally characterized to validate the concept.

The target audience of this book includes researchers, academicians, and application engineers in the field of RF and microwave engineering; as well as researchers and industry personnel in the law enforcement, healthcare, biomedical and defense, and military sectors.

The authors give their respect to Professor James Lin at the University of Illinois at Chicago and Professor Jenshan Lin at the University of Florida, Gainesville, who pioneered the research of radar-based non-invasive human vital sign detection. The authors also acknowledge our anonymous reviewers for providing valuable insight on this proposal. Their valuable comments and suggestions helped us to improve the readability of the book. Further, the authors wish to acknowledge the valuable discussion with their colleagues at IIT Roorkee, India, and Dr. B.A. at the Technological University, Maharashtra, India. In addition, the contribution of students who worked in the RFIC Laboratory at IIT Roorkee is greatly acknowledged.

Brijesh Iyer
Nagendra Prasad Pathak

Authors

Dr. Brijesh Iyer works as an assistant professor in the Department of Electronics and Telecommunication Engineering at the Dr. B.A. Technological University-Lonere-Maharashtra-India (The State Technological University). He completed his doctoral degree in RF and communication engineering in 2015 from the Radio Frequency Integrated Circuit Research Laboratory in the Department of Electronics and Communication Engineering at the Indian Institute of Technology, Roorkee, India. He won Best Paper at the First IEEE MTT-S International Microwave and Radio Frequency Conference (IMaRC-2013) held in New Delhi, India, in December 2013.

Dr. Iyer was the recipient of the INAE Research Fellowship in engineering from 2015 to 2016. He has authored two books and published several papers in international journals and conferences of repute. His research interests include the design and development of concurrent multiband RF circuits and systems for humanitarian applications, allied signal processing, and IoT-based sensor design.

Dr. Nagendra Prasad Pathak works as an associate professor in the Department of Electronics and Communication Engineering at the Indian Institute of Technology, Roorkee, in Uttarakhand, India. He earned a B.Tech. in electronics and telecommunication engineering and an M.Tech. in electronics engineering from the University of Allahabad in 1998 and 1996, respectively. He completed his PhD in the area of millimeter-wave integrated circuits from the Indian Institute of Technology, Delhi, in 2005. Prior to his current assignment to IIT Roorkee in 2006, he held the position of postdoctoral research fellow at the NRD Super Broadband Research Centre, Tohoku Institute of Technology, Sendai, Japan, as well as at the Centre for Applied Research in Electronics (CARE), IIT, Delhi. Dr. Pathak was invited by the Indian National Academy of Engineering (INAE) to deliver a talk at the 9th National Frontiers of Engineering Symposium for Young Indian Engineers held at Jodhpur (June 2015). He is the recipient of the DST Fast Track Research Grant for Young Scientists (2007); the IETE India National Research Fellowship in the area of microwave and radar engineering (2004, 2005); and the Junior Research Fellowship through DRDO, Government of India, in the area of integrated optics (1999).

Dr. Pathak has served as vice chairman of the IEEE Microwave Theory and Techniques Society (MTT-S), Uttar Pradesh Chapter (2014 to 2016); faculty advisor, IEEE MTT-S IIT Roorkee student branch (2011 to present); and coordinator of student activities and member of the executive committee of the IEEE Uttar Pradesh section (2015 to 2016). Dr. Pathak has acted as a reviewer of the *IEEE Sensor Journal*; *IEEE Photonics Technology Letters*; *IEEE Microwave &*

Wireless Component Letters; IEEE Antennas and Wireless Propagation Letters; IEEE Transactions on Wireless Communications; IEEE Transactions on Geoscience & Remote Sensing; Electronic Letters; Journal of Infrared, Millimeter, and Terahertz Waves; and International Journal of RF & Microwave Computer Aided Engineering.

Dr. Pathak has guided six PhD theses and supervised 30 M. Tech dissertations in the area of RF to THz integrated circuits, systems, and sensors. He has published more than 110 papers in reputed international journals and conferences and has one U.S. patent to his credit. Dr. Pathak's current research interests include linear and nonlinear integrated circuits and systems at RF to THz frequencies; non-invasive RF sensors for industrial, defense, civil infrastructure, agriculture, and veterinary applications; intelligent transportation systems; and RF-inspired nanoscale circuits using the concept of spoof plasmonics/graphene plasmonics for RF to THz wireless systems.

1

Introduction

1.1 Introduction: Background and Driving Forces

Recently, thousands of people have lost their lives due to heavy flooding and landslides in Sri Lanka and the hilly area of Uttarakhand, India. Similar situations were reported in Japan, where thousands of people were buried under debris from frequent earthquakes. Under these conditions, the quick search-and-rescue operation was negatively affected due to a lack of suitable portable wireless sensors to ascertain human life under the debris as the electric power supply system, roads, and communication networks in those regions were destroyed due to natural calamity. The necessity of wireless and non-invasive sensors in such a situation was heavily felt by the rescue team as well as the research community.

Another important application scenario is in southern Asia, where a large number of unattended and uncovered bore well pits are the cause of human life disasters. Due to a lack of literacy and awareness, young children often fall inside these, which can be fatal. With existing rescue mechanisms, one cannot ascertain life until the rescue operation is over. With a wireless non-invasive sensor, it may be possible to keep track of human life during the rescue operation, thereby guiding the rescue team to decide its course of action.

A wireless and non-invasive sensor may also be useful in a variety of applications, such as through-the-wall detection for the presence of human beings, remote monitoring of patients' health in hospitals and infant care units, for ascertaining the life of wounded soldiers in battlefields, for the home care of elderly people, in structural health monitoring systems, and to decide the viability of a particular construction.

Motivated from these day-to-day life requirements, this book reports the design and development of a handheld portable wireless sensor to detect the existence of human life non-invasively. The presence of human life is ascertained by the virtue of vital signs such as respiration rate and heartbeat. Hence, they are used as vital signs to indicate the existence of a human life by the proposed sensor. For successful deployment of the device as a sensor for the aforementioned applications, it must fulfill the various criteria:

- The device should be sensitive and capable of detecting even a minute variation of human vital signs.
- The prediction accuracy of the device must be very high, that is, it should be robust against any variation in the measurement conditions.
- The device should be portable enough to be easily carried from one place to another.
- The power consumption of the device should be minimum.
- Most importantly, the device must be cost-effective and reproducible.

As per the records available in the literature, efforts were initiated in the early 1970s toward the non-invasive detection of human vital signs using radio frequency (RF) systems. In 1975, RF systems were used for the first time in the assessment of vital signs of human beings and animals [1]. The high-sensitivity and miniaturized RF systems based on the Doppler principle have been employed as wireless sensors in numerous day-to-day applications; for example, in sleep disorder detection, location and distance estimation, detection of food contamination, characterization of materials and substances, and human vital sign detection in battlefields and sports fields [2–7], among others. These systems have also been found to be very useful by law enforcement agencies to inflict through-the-wall human detection and direction of arrival estimation and in hospitals for non-invasive human healthcare monitoring. Recently, the sensors based on the radar principle have been employed for structural health monitoring [8–13].

However, most of these reported systems are focused on the use of a particular single-band radio or instrument-based bulky systems. The challenging issue in the reported systems is the compromise between the detection sensitivity and the noise content in the signals. This factor has hindered the deployment of such systems as a portable sensor with high detection accuracy. In view of this, the book reports on the design, development, and analysis of a concurrent dualband RF sensor for remote monitoring of human vital signs to detect and ascertain the presence of human life. Figure 1.1 depicts the motivation for development of a non-invasive RF sensor.

1.2 Theory of Non-Invasive VSD Radar

Vital signs are the symptoms of physiological information, frequently used to evaluate the fundamental body functionality. In healthcare terminology, measurements of vital signs are classified into two types: in vivo (on or within a human body) and in vitro (exterior of human body) [18]. Measurement of vital signs, in principle, involves recording of heartbeat

(a)

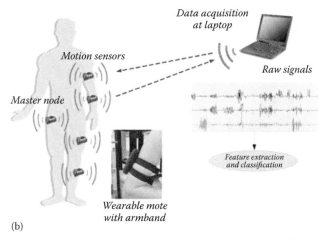

(b)

FIGURE 1.1
Motivation for the book: (a) Disaster management, (b) healthcare applications.   (*Continued*)

and respiration rate, body temperature, and blood pressure. Among these, the respiration rate and heartbeat are more significantly used vital signs to predict physical health of a human being since a close nonlinear relation exists between the respiratory and the cardiovascular systems. Both the heartbeat and respiration rate are modified by the target activity (i.e., the human being).

Vital signs vary continuously with the age of the human being. In general, measurement of the human vital signs may be principally carried out by either using the bioelectric energy generated within the cardiac muscle

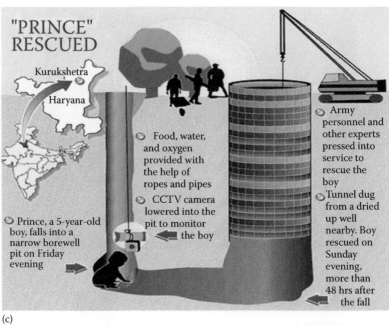

(c)

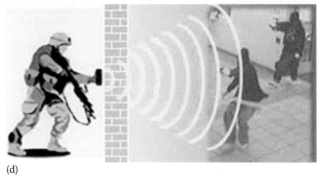

(d)

FIGURE 1.1 (CONTINUED)
Motivation for the book: (c) social aspects, (d) battlefields and law enforcement applications. (From U Turn Foundation, Rehabilitation of Villages Devastated in Uttarakhand Flood, http://uturnfoundation.org/wputurn/rehabilitation-of-villages-devastated-in-uttarakhand -flood [14]; CodeBlue Project, http://www.eecs.Harvard.edu/~mdw/proj/codeblue [15]; Prince Rescued, KBK Infographics, http://im.rediff.com/news/2006/jul/23prince.gif [16]; RANGE-R, Theory of Operation, http://www.range-r.com/tech/theory.htm [17].)

(direct method) or measurement of periodic displacement of the chest wall surface due to the heart's contractions (indirect method). The direct method of assessment requires a measuring device capable of detecting changes in the surrounding electric field. The indirect method works on the principle of the Doppler phase shift.

1.2.1 Working Principle

With advancements in technology, the traditional invasive vital sign monitoring systems are becoming less invasive and more sophisticated. RF systems with non-invasive monitoring of respiration and heartbeat provide a choice over well-known invasive techniques. The non-invasive vital sign detection (NIVSD) system works on the principle of change in phase of electromagnetic waves due to partial reflection at the separation of two mediums and propagation all the way through the medium. Such RF-based non-invasive measurement methods neither confine nor cause distress, as conventional vital sign measurement methods do, to the human being. Table 1.1 provides a comparison between the traditional invasive systems and the NIVSD system.

This aspect of non-invasive detection becomes predominantly significant for long-term continuous monitoring of the vital signs of a human being. Radio detection and ranging (radar) is an RF system used for detection of objects with radio waves. Since its first report, radar technology continuously progressed and became established over the decades [19,20]. The RF sensor system for NIVSD is based on radar. It transmits a continuous wave (CW) signal in the medium. This signal is reflected back from the target object which is subsequently received in a receiver.

As per Doppler's principle, an object with a time-varying location produces a phase-modulated reflected signal in proportion to its time-varying location. Thus, an RF system with the chest as a target receives a phase-modulated signal in proportion to the time-varying chest position. Accordingly, a baseband signal having intelligence about the heartbeat and respiration rate can be retrieved after demodulation of the received signal. Based on this theory, a non-invasive heartbeat and respiration rate monitoring system has been developed in the literature illustrated.

1.2.2 Issues with the NIVSD Sensor

For successful deployment of an RF sensor for non-invasive detection of human vital signs, challenges including clutter and phase noise, direct

TABLE 1.1

Comparison of Invasive and Non-Invasive VSD System

VSD System	Invasive	Wireless Detection	Cooperation from Subject	Detection Methodology
Invasive (traditional)	Yes	Not Possible	Essential	Using starchy electrodes
NIVSD	No	Possible	Optional	Using RF Signals

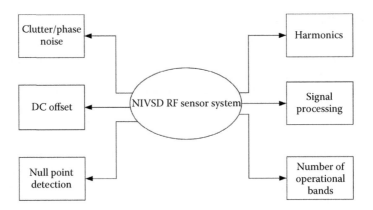

FIGURE 1.2
Challenges associated with a NIVSD RF sensor design. (From Iyer, B., Pathak, N., and Ghosh, D., IEEE Region 10 Humanitarian Technology Conference (R10 HTC), Chennai, India, 112–119, 2014 [21].)

component (DC) offset, null point detection, higher-order harmonics, and appropriate signal-processing techniques need to be addressed. Moreover, the number of operational bands govern the accuracy of detection. Each one of these issues or a combination of multiple issues may demean the total system performance. The evolution of RF system for NIVSD has its roots in unearthing solutions to these challenges. Figure 1.2 shows the challenges associated with the design and deployment of non-invasive RF sensors.

1.2.2.1 Clutters

Clutters are superfluous echoes from innate surroundings. Large clutters may masquerade as echoes from the targets and, in turn, decrease the system capacity. Clutter and phase noise effects may be minimized by using the same local oscillator (LO) source for transmission and reception. Phase noise of the reflected signal is allied with the LO and the degree of association depends on the time lag between the two signals. Smaller delays minimize the baseband noise significantly. This time delay is related to the distance between the RF system and targets, that is, the range of the target. Accordingly, this phase noise reduction is recognized as the range correlation effect [2]. Owing to the impact of clutters over the sensitivity of detection of very minute vital sign signals, several techniques have been proposed to overcome the effect of clutters, as discussed in the following chapters.

1.2.2.2 DC Offset

DC offset results from receiver limitations, clutters, and DC information related to target location and its allied phase. Due to random body movements, the DC component may be significant compared with the AC signal, which adversely affects the resolution during digitization. The frequency of the detected signal in an NIVSD system is generally between 0.1 Hz to 2 Hz in the baseband spectrum. This is in close proximity to the DC voltage. Hence, the effect of DC offset is extremely significant in an NIVSD system. This DC offset can be effectively minimized with the help of proper receiver architecture.

1.2.2.3 Null Point Detection

The performance of an NIVSD system is largely governed by the phenomenon of null point and optimal point. The sensitivity of the system is decreased when the detected signal is proportional to the second (or higher) order of the chest displacement signal instead of the displacement itself. As a result, the fundamental component of chest wall displacement is decreased and the overall sensitivity of the system is decreased. This is recognized as the null point problem in NIVSD. When the baseband signal is proportional to the irregular chest movement, conceivable phase demodulation sensitivity is attained. This is the optimum point. The adjacent null point and optimum point are always $\lambda/8$ distance apart from each other [11]. Figure 1.3 depicts the concept of the occurrence of a null point and the optimum point. The accurate detection of human vital signs is possible only with negligible null point effect. Due to its importance, many efforts have been initiated by researchers to overcome the null point problem.

1.2.2.4 Higher-Order Harmonics

In general, the amplitude of the respiration signal is greater than (even more than 10 times) the amplitude of the heartbeat. Therefore, the baseband signal cannot be considered linear when displacement due to respiration is adequately large. As a consequence, dominant higher-order harmonics will emerge in the region of the heartbeat frequency. The blocking effect of higher-order harmonics decreases the accuracy of heartbeat detection.

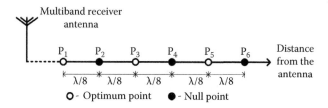

FIGURE 1.3
Illustration of optimum and null points. (Adapted from Xiao, Y., Lin, J., Lubecke, O., and Lubecke, V., *IEEE Transaction on Microwave Theory and Techniques*, 54, 5, 2023–2032, 2006 [11].)

1.2.2.5 *Signal Processing*

Radar signal processing aims to reduce false alarms and improve the signal-to-noise ratio (SNR). For processing the baseband signal, in general, all NIVSDs use the simple fast Fourier transform (FFT) technique. Recently, wavelet transform (WT) has also been used in the analysis of NIVSD. A comparative study between the FFT and WT shows that the WT is a better alternative for NIVSD analysis [22]. The RELAX algorithm, a parametric and cyclic improvement approach, least squares method, method of correlation, maximum likelihood (ML) estimations, and principal component analysis (PCA)–based adaptive filter algorithms are also used to estimate respiration and heartbeat parameters [23–24].

Further, various other signal-processing techniques for the extraction of human vital signs have been reported, such as Kalman filters, blind source separation, preservation of DC information, and fast clutter cancellation methods [25–28]. Recently, Chirp Z-transform (CZT) has been proposed as an alternative to FFT. It is a simplification of the Z-transform that achieves better resolution even without expanding the number of specimens [29]. Statistical signal-processing and MIMO adaption can also be alternatives to the existing signal-processing techniques. From the available literature, it may be inferred that NIVSD technology has matured enough on the signal processing front.

1.2.2.6 *Number of Operational Bands*

For human vital sign detection, detection sensitivity and accuracy are the challenging issues. The existing technology for the RF NIVSD systems is based on the operation of a particular single band. These systems can either provide detection sensitivity or accuracy at the cost of each other. Hence, the operational band employed for detection is a key for successful deployment of such systems as a sensor.

1.3 Scope of the Book

This book aims to report the design and development of a concurrent dual-band RF sensor system operating simultaneously at 2.44 GHz and 5.25 GHz frequency bands for non-invasive human vital sign detection. The implementation of the proposed sensor requires the design and characterization of concurrent dualband subsystems such as patch antenna arrays, low noise amplifiers, Wilkinson power divider/combiners, and oscillators. An efficient signal-processing algorithm for the accurate detection of human vital signs is also required. Application of the proposed sensor as an occupancy sensor can be verified by estimating the direction of arrival (DoA) so that the position of the human being can be confirmed.

1.4 About This Book

Recently non-invasive RF sensors have drawn considerable attention from the industry and academia. Many researchers and academicians are working in this area and have contributed toward the development of non-invasive RF sensors. However, this book provides a collective information for the design and development of a multiband non-invasive RF sensor.

Chapter 2 presents the basics of radio architecture, its classification, and the fundamentals of the radar system. Further, a review on the state-of-the-art of the proposed RF sensor is discussed herein. The challenges and limitations in the design and implementation of RF sensors for NIVSD applications are discussed. The literature review provides a pathway to arrive at the conclusion that there is a need for significant improvement in the present-day technology for non-invasive detection of human vital signs.

Chapter 3 describes the design and characterization of the radiating elements used in the proposed NIVSD sensor. The gain and directivity are the two prime factors governing the selection of a particular antenna. Additionally, low-cost, lightweight, and ease in reproduction are considered to be the design goals before initiating the design. Out of the several antenna structures available in the literature, low-cost concurrent dualband microstrip patch antenna array structures have been developed to operate simultaneously at 2.44 GHz and 5.25 GHz for the proposed sensor.

Chapter 4 of the book describes the design and characterization of the RF front-end subsystems of the proposed sensor. As a part of the front end, two oscillators have been developed to operate at 2.44 GHz and 5.25 GHz. Further, a concurrent dualband Wilkinson power divider/combiner and an LNA that simultaneously operates at the 2.44 GHz and 5.25 GHz frequency bands have been designed, fabricated, and characterized using hybrid MIC technology.

Chapter 5 describes the characterization of the concurrent dualband NIVSD sensor for human vital sign detection. A unified concurrent dualband sensor system is developed using the subsystems described in Chapters 3 and 4. The signal-processing method applied to the baseband signals to extract the desired respiration rate and heartbeat signal is discussed therein. Safety considerations, link budget, and link margin analysis are also carried out in support of the proposed sensor.

Chapter 6 describes the application of the concurrent dualband sensor as an occupancy and position sensor. The detection and location of a human being inside a room is carried out with the help of the proposed sensor.

The concurrent dualband operation for deciding the occupancy reduces the dead spots and false alarms in the detection process. It is found that the proposed mechanism works best up to a distance of 2 meters. Further, the location of a human being is ascertained by estimating the direction of arrival of RF signals.

Chapter 7 concludes the book with a discussion on the capacity of the proposed concurrent dualband RF sensor for non-invasive human vital sign detection. The future scope of the proposed work is also discussed therein.

1.5 Concluding Remarks

The chapter described the motivation behind the present book along with the theory and working principle of a human VSD radar. In addition, the various technical issues which may affect the workings of a human VSD are discussed herein. As a concluding remark, this part of the book presents the basics of a non-invasive human VSD system and paves the pathway for the design of a new non-invasive RF sensor for human vital sign detection.

2

Preliminaries and Review

2.1 Introduction

The initial discussion in Chapter 1 paved the way for the design and development of an NIVSD sensor for human vital sign detection. Since their first report in the 1970s, contactless human vital sign detection system has drawn the attention of researchers and academicians due to attractive features such as non-invasiveness, low cost, and ability to perform long-term monitoring of human vital signs.

This chapter presents the state-of-the-art advancements in the technology for the design and development of a non-invasive RF sensor for human vital sign detection. The chapter has been divided into two parts. The first part describes topologies used for NIVSD applications, while the second part describes various measures reported in the literature to overcome the challenges encountered during the NIVSD operation, as discussed in Chapter 1. Based on the available literature, research gaps are also discussed in this chapter.

2.2 Radio Architecture

The present era of electronics engineering is of product development with features like compact in size, has low power consumption, and is robust against noise. Radio frequency integrated circuit (RFIC) design is an exciting area for research for product development. With the constant and rapid development in the technologies, the bulky and discrete circuits can now be integrated onto a single chip. Day-to-day life applications, such as cordless phones and cell phones, wireless local area networks (WLANs), keyless entry for cars, wireless toll collection, global positioning system (GPS) navigation, remote tags, asset tracking, remote sensing, tuners in cable modems, and so on, require RFICs in their design and deployment as commercial products.

This huge increase in interest in radio frequency (RF) communications has drawn the attention of academia and industry to provide complete systems on an integrated circuit (IC). In academia, the research has been undertaken with an aim to design a complete radio on one chip.

From a more technical point of view, quality is often measured in terms of bit error rate, and acceptable quality might be to experience less than one error in every million bits. Cost can be seen as the price of the communications equipment or the need to replace or recharge batteries. Low cost implies simple circuits to minimize circuit area, but also low power dissipation to maximize battery life.

Owing to these facts, multiband, multifunctional RFICs have become popular in the present era. Such radios are capable of operating simultaneously at two or more designated bands. These radios are designed on a component sharing basis in which the same hardware operates at different designated bands. The multifunctional radios can be designed using parallel arrangements of front-end circuits, by using a control switch to swing between the designated bands and the concurrent operation.

2.2.1 Transmitter Architecture

The design and development of RF transmitters for wireless applications is challenging due to its various considerations, such as number of components, the interference, output power requirements, and so on, which play the major role in deciding on a particular transmitter topology. Further, the number of oscillators and filters may also affect the choice of a specific transmitter topology.

2.2.1.1 Direct Conversion Architecture

This architecture of a radio transmitter is very simple in its construction. Here, the output frequency is equal to the local oscillator frequency. However, this architecture badly suffers from the phenomenon of injection pulling, despite the shielding techniques [30]. This phenomenon can be overcome by isolating the power amplifier (PA) spectrum from the oscillator frequency. Figure 2.1 shows a typical direct conversion transmitter.

2.2.1.2 The Two-Step Architecture

The phenomenon of LO pulling in transmitters can be overcome by upconverting the baseband signals in two steps. This methodology keeps the PA spectrum far away from the frequencies of VCOs [31]. Figure 2.2 shows a typical two-stage transmitter.

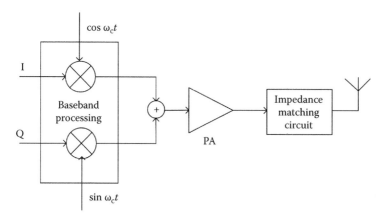

FIGURE 2.1
A typical direct conversion transmitter. (Adapted from Razavi, B., IEEE Custom Integrated Circuits Conference, pp. 197–204, 1999 [31].)

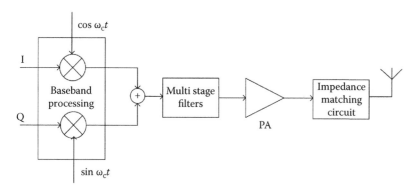

FIGURE 2.2
A typical two-stage transmitter. (Adapted from Razavi, B., IEEE Custom Integrated Circuits Conference, pp. 197–204, 1999 [31].)

2.2.1.3 Offset PLL Architecture

A transmitter topology employed in the systems with constant envelope modulation is the offset PLL architecture. This architecture was evolved to fulfill the stringent GSM requirements of the thermal noise in the receiver operational bands [32]. Figure 2.3 shows a typical PLL architecture.

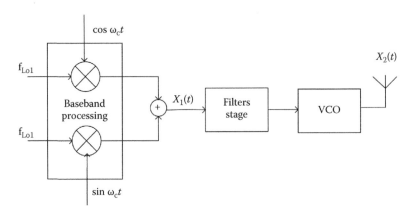

FIGURE 2.3
PLL transmitter architecture. (Adapted from Razavi, B., IEEE Custom Integrated Circuits Conference, pp. 197–204, 1999 [31].)

2.2.1.4 The Multiband Multifunction Transmitter

This type of transmitter architecture is specially designed to support many operation bands simultaneously with the same circuitry. This is also known as *modern age architecture*. These circuits are based on hardware sharing and the same circuits can be used to operate concurrently at different designated bands. Due to this phenomenon the front end becomes very compact with fewer power requirements.

2.2.2 Receiver Architecture

The amplifiers, mixers, filters, and oscillators are the main components of any receiver architecture. The receiver architecture can be classified as follows.

2.2.2.1 Homodyne Receiver Architecture

This is also known as a *direct conversion receiver* (DCR) or a *zero IF receiver*. This architecture is very popular due to its simple circuitry as it converts only a single frequency at a time. In this architecture of radio receiver, the incoming radio signal is demodulated using synchronous detection driven by a local oscillator whose frequency is similar to, or very close to, the carrier frequency of the received signal. Figure 2.4 shows a block diagram of homodyne receiver architecture.

The fundamental advantage of this architecture is that it does not have image bands, and hence, the allied RF-filtering is not so critical. Further, it doesn't have many spurious responses. However, this architecture may suffer due to difficulties in implementation such as dc offsets and leakage between receivers and transmitters in full duplex operation. The direct

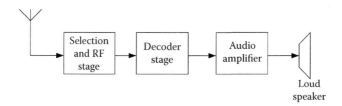

FIGURE 2.4
Block diagram of homodyne receiver architecture.

conversion principle has become quite popular in recent years in mobile terminals. This is mostly due to the availability of effective digital calibration/compensation methods.

2.2.2.2 Heterodyne Receiver Architecture

A superheterodyne radio receiver was invented by U.S. engineer Edwin Armstrong in 1918 during World War I [33]. It is a type of radio receiver in which the received signal frequency is converted to a fixed intermediate frequency (IF) by using frequency mixing. Such a conversion is carried out for more convenient processing than the original carrier frequency. Virtually all modern radio receivers use the superheterodyne principle.

However, it also suffers from drawbacks, such as high power consumptions difficulty in the integration of some parts like IF/RF filters, and oscillators, complicated structure, and spurious responses. Figure 2.5 depicts the heterodyne radio receiver.

2.2.2.3 Multifunctional Receiver Architecture

The homodyne or heterodyne architecture supports only single-band operation. However, the recent developments in RFICs requires compact radios with low power consumption and multiband operations. This requirement can be achieved by using a multifunctional receiver architecture wherein

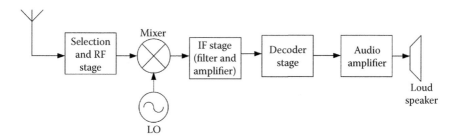

FIGURE 2.5
The heterodyne radio receiver.

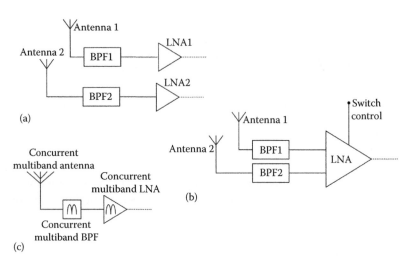

FIGURE 2.6
Multifunctional radio receiver architecture.

single-band radio architecture supports the multiband operations. This architecture can be devised by using a homodyne or heterodyne architecture. Figure 2.6 depicts a typical multifunctional radio receiver architecture.

2.3 State-of-the-Art NIVSD Radar

The working principle of a non-invasive RF sensor for human vital sign detection is illustrated in Figure 2.7. Here $S_{inc}(t)$ is the transmitted signal, $S_{ref}(t)$ is the received signal, ϕ is the phase variation between $S_{inc}(t)$ and $S_{ref}(t)$, L is the distance between the RF sensor and the target, and $\Delta\phi(t)$ is

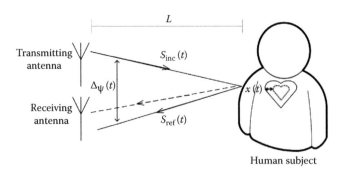

FIGURE 2.7
Working principle of a non-invasive RF sensor for human vital sign detection.

the total phase noise due to signal source and subsystems of the transmitter. The baseband signal $S_B(t)$ is obtained after demodulating the received signal. Let the transmitted signal $S_{inc}(t)$ be a sinusoidal wave with frequency f. Then

$$S_{inc}(t) = \cos[2\pi f t + \phi(t)] \tag{2.1}$$

If a target (a human body) is at a distance L from the transmitter and has a chest disarticulation $x(t)$, then the total distance between the transmitter and the receiver is $2L(t) = 2L + 2x(t)$. According to [2], the received signal can subsequently be approximated as

$$S_{ref}(t) \cong \cos\left[2\pi f t - \frac{4\pi L}{\lambda} - \frac{4\pi x(t)}{\lambda} - \phi\left(t - \frac{2L}{c}\right)\right] \tag{2.2}$$

where c is transmission velocity of the signal, λ is signal wavelength in air, and $\phi[t - (2L/c)]$ is the phase noise contributed by the medium noise and the source.

From Equation 2.2, it can be inferred that the received signal is analogous to the transmitted signal, except that it has a time lag equal to the sum of the target distance and the phase modulation due to the irregular movement of the target (human being). Information about the irregular chest movement can be retrieved by demodulating the received signal. The consequential baseband signal $S_B(t)$ obtained after demodulation is estimated as [2]

$$S_B(t) \cong \cos\left[\frac{4\pi L}{\lambda} + \frac{4\pi x(t)}{\lambda} + \phi + \Delta\phi(t)\right] \tag{2.3}$$

$$\Delta\phi(t) = \phi(t) - \phi\left[t - \frac{2L}{c}\right] \tag{2.4}$$

where $[4\pi L/\lambda]$ is a phase shift due to distance L of the target, ϕ is a phase shift due to the surface reflection and delay caused in the subsystems, and $\Delta\phi(t)$ is the residual phase noise.

It is difficult to devise a specific model to describe a human chest displacement. This is because the heart and lungs undergo complex movements inside the thorax. The displacement due to this results in amplitude and phase variation at different areas of the chest surface. In addition, the heartbeat and respiration rates for human being vary with age and other physiological conditions. However, from a monitoring point of view, it is sufficient to know whether the subject's heartbeat and respiration rates are normal or due to irregular chest displacement. Owing to all these facts, the heartbeat and respiration can be symbolized as the sum of two sinusoidal waves with heartbeat and respiration rates as their respective frequencies. Then, the signals due to the respiration rate is approximated as

$$x_{resp}(t) = a_{resp} \cos\left(2\pi f_{resp}(t)\right) \qquad (2.5)$$

where $x_{resp}(t)$ is the displacement of chest due to respiration, a_{resp} is the amplitude of the displacement of respiration and f_{resp} is the respiratory frequency. The signals due to the heartbeats are approximated as

$$x_{hb}(t) = a_{hb} \cos\left(2\pi f_{hb}(t)\right) \qquad (2.6)$$

where $x_{hb}(t)$ is the chest displacement due to heartbeat, a_{hb} is the amplitude of the displacement of heartbeat, and f_{hb} is the heartbeat frequency. The overall displacement due to the heartbeat and respiration is approximated as

$$x(t) = x_{resp}(t) + x_{hb}(t) \qquad (2.7)$$

Equations 2.1 to 2.7 indicate that the NIVSD sensor measures only the disparity on the surface of the chest wall. As a result, the amplitude of the detected signals heavily depends on the physiological structure of the subject under test. Table 2.1 summarizes the parameters of the two vital sign signals of a human being with a normal physique as per the American Heart Association (AHA). These parameters are considered for all the experimentation analysis in this book.

2.3.1 Radar Architecture

In case of invasive detection of human vital signs, the conventional electrodes are used, which not only gives a starchy feeling to the users but also suffers from the need for periodic maintenance. In the non-invasive detection of human vital signs, radios based on the Doppler phase shift are used in which the microwave-sensing systems transmit a RF, single-tone CW signal, which is reflected from the target and then demodulated in the receiver. Demodulation

TABLE 2.1

Summary of Human Vital Sign as per AHA Standard

Activity	Bits/Minute	Frequency(Hz)
Respiration rate	10–24	0.16–0.4
Heartbeats	60–100	1–1.67

Source: Target Heart Rates, American Heart Association, available at http://www.heart.org/HEARTORG /GettingHealthy.

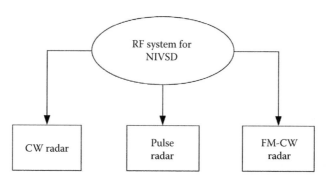

FIGURE 2.8
Radar topologies.

provides a signal corresponding to the human chest wall position that contains information about the movement due to heartbeat and respiration.

This technique enables noncontact detection of vital signs of humans or animals from a distance without any sensor physically attached to the body. The measurements may be carried out by using different radar topologies. Figure 2.8 represents the different radar topologies involved in typical NIVSD applications.

2.3.1.1 CW Doppler Radar

In the CW radar approach, the transmitted signal itself is used as the local oscillator signal in the down conversion process. Due to this, the baseband signal does not suffer from any frequency offset problem and the associated time delays. Hence, it directly eliminates the requirement of a synchronizing mechanism. The CW radar radio approach has drawn the interest of researchers primarily due to its simple architecture, low power requirement, and clutter cancellation with proper front-end arrangement [23,34]. A MIMO technique for detection of multiple movements and target tracking can be implemented with ease using a CW radar. The front-end architectures for the non-invasive detection of human vital signs include direct conversion or zero IF receiver, heterodyne radios, double side band radios, direct IF sampling radio, and a self-injection locking architecture [35–37].

2.3.1.2 UWB Radar

With a UWB pulse radar, a very short electromagnetic pulse is transmitted toward the target. The topologies used to build a UWB pulse radar are described by Immoreev and Tao [38]. The principal advantage of a UWB pulse radar is its ability to eliminate the multipath reflections and clutters. However, it suffers from the need for recalibrations when the distance between radio and object changes.

2.3.1.3 FMCW Radar

Recently, the FMCW radar has been investigated and used in human vital sign detection applications [39]. It transmits a chirp signal for a certain interval. The received ricochets are mixed with the transmitted chirp signal to produce the desired signal with the help of a low-pass filter. In comparison to the traditional pulse radar, FMCW radars have better sensitivity, low power consumption, and higher clutter rejection capacity.

2.3.1.4 Interferometric CW Radar

It employs CW radars operating at different frequencies for human vital sign–sensing applications. Particular radars are selected by an RF-switching mechanism, combined by a combiner. On the receiver side, an RF splitter is used to distinguish between individual band signals. This topology enhances the target detection probability in a highly cluttered environment without increasing the RF spectrum requirement by transitioning to a multicarrier interrogating signal [40].

2.3.1.5 On-Chip Integrated Radar

Developments in the early 2000s have demonstrated the feasibility of integrating this function into modern wireless communication devices operating in L and S bands [41]. The first integrated vital sign radar sensor chip using silicon CMOS has earlier been demonstrated by Droitcour et al. in [42]. The chip integrates all the RF circuits, including a free-running oscillator that provides the transmission signal and also serves as the reference [2].

2.3.2 Methods for Performance Enhancement

As discussed in Chapter 1, an NIVSD sensor for human vital sign detection suffers from various technical issues, such as clutters, DC offsets, null point, and higher-order harmonics. For effective detection of weak human vital signs, these issues must be addressed. Many efforts have been initiated to improve these issues.

2.3.2.1 Clutter and Phase Noise

A microprocessor-based clutter cancellation system was proposed by Chen et al. [43]. In this approach, the microprocessor reduces the DC in the transmitted and received signal by regulating the phase delay and attenuation. The system generates an optimal signal (where the DC level of combined signal is minimum) to eliminate clutters from the surroundings. It also alleviates null point setback. The 1150 MHz microwave life detection system is

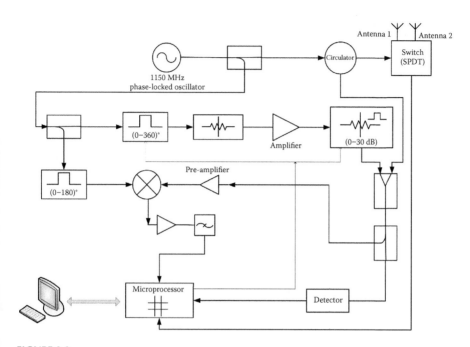

FIGURE 2.9
1150 MHz microwave life detection system. (Adapted from Chen, K., Huang, Y., Zhang, J., and Norman, A., *IEEE Transaction on Biomedical Engineering*, 47, 1, pp. 105–114, 2000 [43].)

shown in Figure 2.9. The major drawback of this system is its bulky hardware size and additional circuitry requirement.

The multiple-input multiple-output (MIMO) technique was used to solve the problem of noise elimination due to random body movement [44]. The individual RF subsystems contribute noise in an NIVSD system. Yu et al. evaluated the detector subsystems individually and collectively to figure the overall noise performance of the detector. Further, the authors carried out experiments for the analysis of tradeoff between output SNR and detection distance [45].

A 60-GHz millimeter wave life detection system (MLDS) was developed at National Cheng Kung University, Taiwan [46]. In this system, a clutter canceller was incorporated with an adjustable attenuator and phase shifter. It effectively reduced clutter from transmitting power leakage and background reflections up to a distance of 2 meters. A synchronized motion technique (SMT) based on the Doppler concept was reported by Cheng et al. of National Taiwan University, Taipei, Taiwan [24]. SMT was used to suppress the interference from the respiration in noncontact heartbeat detection. The experimentation proved that SMT effectively improved the heartbeat-to-respiration ratio (HRR) up to 76 percent in subjects with normal breathing. Use of impulse ratio UWB radar along with a moving averaging filter has been proposed for suppressing clutter arising from random body movement [47]. Thus, all these efforts improved the performance of the existing NIVSD system by alleviating the effect of clutters.

2.3.2.2 DC Offset

DC offset can be effectively minimized with the help of indirect conversion receiver architecture, arctangent demodulation in quadrature receivers, and by double sideband indirect conversion radio architecture [48–50]. The cancellation of noise, caused by the random walking of the human being and the DC offset problem in NIVSD, were further improved by using a Doppler radar array approach. A compensation algorithm was also introduced by Yu et al. to diminish the disturbance of DC offset [51].

An instrumentation Doppler radar system using laboratory equipment was proposed by Gu et al. In this approach, heterodyne digital quadrature demodulation architecture is used to mitigate the inequality in the quadrature channel and need of a complex DC offset calibration in arctangent demodulation [52]. Figure 2.10 shows the block diagram of the instrumentation radar.

2.3.2.3 Null Point Detection

In low-power ultra-wideband (UWB) radar, the I/Q demodulator to acquire two baseband signals in quadrature is an effective mechanism to eliminate the null point problem [2,53]. Thus, the UWB radar mechanism is free from the null point problem. However, a time discriminator with quick-acting switches is solicited to select the preferred reflected pulses. With the I/Q demodulator approach, at least one signal will be at an optimum point. This architecture is less complicated than that reported in [1]. However, this

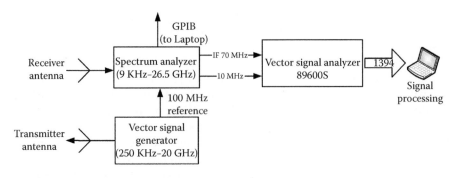

FIGURE 2.10
Block diagram of an instrumental radar system. (Adapted from C., Gu, C., Li, C., Lin, J., Long, J., Huangfu, J., and Ran, L., *IEEE Transaction on Instrumentation and Measurement*, 59, 6, pp. 1580–1588, 2010 [52].)

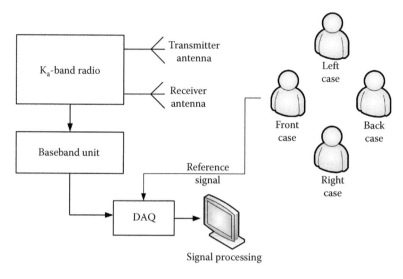

FIGURE 2.11

K$_a$-band transceiver for NIVSD from four sides of the human subject. (Adapted from Li, C., Xiao, Y., and Lin, J., *IEEE Transaction on Microwave Theory and Techniques*, 54, 12, pp. 4464–4471, 2006 [54].)

method suffers from the drawback of the double baseband and signal processing part due to the use of separate I/Q channels.

By keeping double sideband waves at the transmitter output in quadrature, the effect of null point can be minimized [11]. A similar concept was analyzed to overcome the null point problem by Li et al. [54]. Figure 2.11 shows the K$_a$-band transceiver for vital sign detection from four sides of the human subject under test. Direct conversion quadrature architecture, ray-tracing techniques, spectrum analysis, phase diversity, and frequency diversity techniques that act as alternative approaches to I/Q demodulation and double sideband transmission are also used to overcome the null detection problem [2,8,38,55,56].

2.3.2.4 Higher-Order Harmonics

Complex signal and arctangent demodulation and tunable phase shifter direct conversion transceivers may be used to minimize the effect of random body movement [8]. At high carrier frequencies, harmonics and intermodulation interference are eliminated with the help of arctangent demodulation. A comprehensive analysis of the combined effect of sensitivity, null points, and DC offset was carried out in [57]. A multifrequency radar system with a signal correlation function provides a significant improvement in detection sensitivity of human VSD [58]. The main drawback in this approach is the need for a switching mechanism to toggle between the individual bands. The switching delay incorporates variation in the respiration and heartbeats over time. The methodology proposed by Chioukh et al. [58] may be a boon to the modernization of NIVSD sensors if these drawbacks are eliminated.

2.4 Research Gaps in the Existing NIVSD Sensors

An NIVSD sensor must be able to sense very minute physiological displacement in the millimeter or centimeter ranges. Hence, the existence of arbitrary body displacement and different physical conditions can considerably affect the detection sensitivity of NIVSD sensors. Also, for people who have a wider chest displacement due to gasping, system-supporting lower frequency is superior, and vice versa.

From the available literature and reported systems, it is observed that the existing NIVSD sensor operates with a particular single band. With such sensors, detection sensitivity and minimum noise content can be attained at the cost of each other. The challenging issue in front of the existing single-band NIVSD sensor is to bridge the trade-off between the sensitivity and the noise in the detected baseband signal. Hence, a new methodology is necessary to minimize this trade-off, thereby improving the performance of the existing NIVSD sensors.

The performance of the existing single-band NIVSD sensors can be improved by using multiband operation. A higher frequency allows signal detection even with very minute variations, but at the cost of increased noise whereas lower frequencies minimize noise but with decreased detection sensitivity. Multiband systems can reap the advantage of increased detection sensitivity with lower noise interference. A multiband architecture can be achieved by parallel, switchable, or concurrent arrangement of transceiver building blocks. The use of parallel system architecture for concurrent operation at individual frequency bands is less attractive due to the requirements for high power consumption, large hardware, and its bulky nature. Detection from either side of the human body by two separate transceivers is unappealing due to its hardware requirements [55]. A switched mode multiband system has the drawback of inconsistent measurement conditions for the same human subject due to switching delay [58]. Further, multifrequency interferometric radar is used for this purpose where selection of frequency is incorporated by means of an RF switch. Similar methodologies were proposed by Fletcher and Han and Oum et al. for random body moment cancellation so as to achieve fair detection of the required signals [59,60].

However, all these schemes are not commercially viable due to one or more reasons like the requirements of large hardware, high power consumption, and complex radio architecture. A brief summary of state-of-the-art non-invasive human vital sign detection systems is given in Table 2.2.

The current trend in the area of microwave/millimeter wave integrated circuit research is to reduce system losses, increase compactness, and

TABLE 2.2

The State-of-the-Art NIVSD System as an RF Sensor

Contribution	Number of Operational Bands	Mode of Operation	Size	Subsystem Design Using	Baseband Signal Processing
J.C. Lin [1]	Single band	–	Bulky	Commercial devices	Radio meter output is used
C. Gu et al. [52]	Dualband	Switchable operation by separate antenna for each band	Bulky	Commercial devices	FFT
Chioukh et al. [58]	Three independent bands	Nonconcurrent, individual single-band RF system	Bulky	Commercial devices/ subsystems	FFT
Proposed system	Dualband	Concurrent operation at designated frequencies	Compact	Own customized concurrent dualband subsystems	FFT, WT

reduce the power consumption level so that the RF systems can be used as a portable handheld device. A concurrent multiband system, based on hardware sharing, fulfills all above criteria. Figure 2.12 shows the conceptual diagram of a dualband RF sensor for non-invasive human vital sign detection.

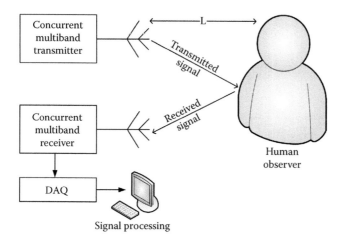

FIGURE 2.12
Conceptual diagram of a multiband RF sensor for NIVSD.

2.5 Concluding Remarks

In this chapter, a brief discussion of the state-of-the-art NIVSD system as an RF sensor for human VSD has been presented. The chapter began with a review on the existing technology for NIVSD sensors and ended with a theoretical background for the proposed work. The available literature clearly elaborate that there is a need of new technology for improving the performance of existing single-band RF sensors for human VSD.

3

Design and Characterization
of the Radiating Elements

3.1 Introduction

An antenna is a device acting as a transition element between the RF front-end circuitry and free space. The advancements in wireless applications and allied consumer services demonstrate the need for a low-cost, compact, and reliable antenna. There are many types of antennas, for example, dipole antennas, monopole antennas, patch antennas, reflector antennas, and horn antennas, which are available for commercial use as well as for other specific applications. The idea of a microstrip antennas was first proposed by Deschamps in 1953 [61]. Since then, a large amount of research has been carried out by researchers and academicians in search of an attractive solution in developing compact, conformal, and low-cost antennas for wireless applications. This chapter describes the design and characterization of a concurrent dualband microstrip patch antennas to fulfill their requirements, such as low cost, lightweight, and reproducibility for use in NIVSD sensor applications.

3.2 Theory of Microstrip Antennas

The microstrip patch antenna consists of a radiating patch on one side of a dielectric substrate and a ground plane on the other side, as shown in Figure 3.1. Here, t is the thickness of the patch; L and W are the length and width of the patch, respectively; and h is the height of the substrate. The patch is generally rectangular, circular, triangular, or elliptical in nature. The radiation pattern of the antennas depends on the surface current distribution of the radiating patch and the feed structure. The impedance matching of the antenna is also sensitive to the feed structure. A variety of mechanisms, such as waveguide feed, microstrip line feed, coplanar waveguide feed, proximity coupling feed, and aperture coupling feed, have been reported in the literature [62].

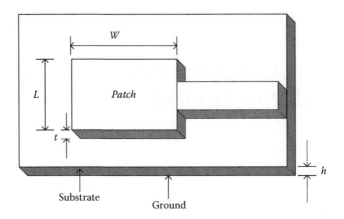

FIGURE 3.1
A microstrip patch structure.

A variety of substrates can be used in the design of a microstrip antenna with a dielectric constant in the range of $2.2 \le \varepsilon_r \le 12$. Substrates whose dielectric constants are at the lower end of this range are mostly prepared as they provide better efficiency and larger bandwidth. The design procedure of a microstrip antenna may be summarized as follows [63]. For efficient radiation, the width W is given by

$$W = \frac{C}{2 f_0 \sqrt{\dfrac{\varepsilon_r}{2}}} \tag{3.1}$$

where ε_r is the dielectric constant of the substrate, h is the height of dielectric substrate and W is the width of the patch. For $f_0 = 2.44$ GHz and $\varepsilon_r = 3.2$, this yields $W = 42.39$ mm. The value of ε_{reff} for microstrip line is computed for substrate height $h = 0.1524$ cm using the following relation:

$$\varepsilon_{reff} = \frac{(\varepsilon_r + 1)}{2} \frac{(\varepsilon_r - 1)}{2} \left[1 + 12\frac{h}{W} \right]^{\frac{-1}{2}} \tag{3.2}$$

It is found that ε_{reff} is 2.67. Then the fringe factor ΔL is calculated as

$$\Delta L = 0.412\,h\,\frac{(\varepsilon_{reff} + 0.3)\left(\dfrac{W}{h} + 0.264\right)}{(\varepsilon_{reff} - 0.258)\left(\dfrac{W}{h} + 0.8\right)} \tag{3.3}$$

The fringe factor ΔL turns out to be 0.075 cm. Finally, the length of the substrate L is calculated as

$$L = L_{eff} + 2\Delta L \tag{3.4}$$

where L_{eff} is the effective length of the patch antenna and expressed for a given resonance frequency as

$$L_{eff} = \frac{C}{2f_o\sqrt{\varepsilon_{reff}}} \tag{3.5}$$

The length of the microstrip line patch is determined to be 36.08 mm. The length and width of the patch are further optimized to obtain the desired results and discussed in Section 3.2.1.2.

For an NIVSD system, a low power, compact, and lightweight antenna is desired. In addition to this, it should be very easy in fabrication with high reproducibility. In this context, a concurrent dualband microstrip patch antenna array is designed and used in the experimentation. The reason behind this particular choice is the extra gain achievement from an array structure. The designed antenna operates simultaneously at 2.44 GHz and 5.25 GHz frequency band. The patch antenna array is designed, fabricated, and characterized to have omnidirectional and directional radiation patterns for use in the proposed sensor. Furthermore, the antenna structure reported by Rathore et al. is modified and experimentally characterized so as to use during experimentation [63].

One of the major factors that differentiate the antenna from others is its radiation pattern. Hypothetically, it is assumed that the isotropic antenna radiates equally in all directions. On the other hand, an omnidirectional antenna has a nondirectional pattern in azimuth and a directional pattern along the direction of elevation. In contrast, a directional antenna is one that has its radiation pattern concentrated in some specific direction only. It inherently acts as a filter for the directions other than it is intended for. The E-plane pattern is defined as the radiation pattern in a plane having the electric field vector and the direction of maximum radiation. The H-plane pattern is the radiation pattern in the plane containing the magnetic field vector and the direction of maximum radiation.

3.3 Characterization of the Concurrent Dualband Patch Antenna

For the purpose of experimentation, the concurrent dualband antenna reported in [63] is modified and optimized or a commercial NH9320 substrate, which is a polytetrafluoroethylene (PTFE)/glass/ceramic dielectric. It has a relative dielectric constant $\varepsilon_r = 3.2$, height $(h) = 1.524$ mm, thickness $(t) = 18$ μm,

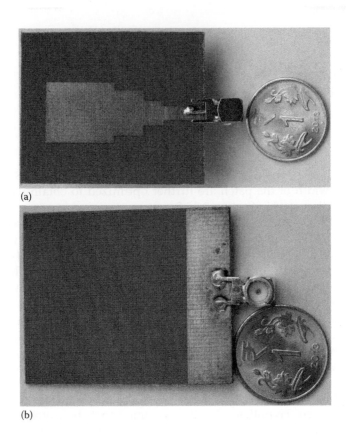

(a)

(b)

FIGURE 3.2
Fabricated prototype of a concurrent dualband patch antenna: (a) Patch side; (b) ground side.

and a loss tangent (σ) = 0.0024. For array design, an omnidirectional and a directional patch antenna have been designed and characterized. The initial patch dimensions are calculated for operation at lower frequency bands and, subsequently, optimization has been carried out to obtain radiation in both the frequency bands. The design of the proposed antennas are simulated and verified with a computer simulation technology (CST-2012) platform by considering a hexahedral mesh element with 20 lines per lambda. The simulated antennas are then fabricated by using the wet etching technique. The design and characterization details has are described in the following sections. Figure 3.2 depicts the fabricated prototype of a concurrent dualband antenna.

3.3.1 Directional 1 × 2 Patch Antenna Array

3.3.1.1 Background

In the past, the development of dualband antennas was initiated in a large extent. Nearly all these antennas are designed for wireless applications with omnidirective radiation pattern. A noncontact vital sign detection-centric approach was proposed by Park and Lin [64,65]. However, these activities end with a broadband performance. Efforts were initiated by researchers to develop a directional array antenna using planar technology. Such a radiation pattern is very useful in healthcare, military, and disaster management applications where the existence of a human being is to be confirmed. A 1 × 2 and a 1 × 4 antenna array were presented by Swelam et al. for operation at 3.5 GHz and 5 GHz bands with separate aperture feedings [66]. A four-element single-band rectangular microstrip patch antenna for a 2.4 GHz application was described by Khraisat [67]. A single-band slotted 2 × 2 microstrip patch antenna array for 5.25 GHz band was reported by Ghosh et al. [68]. A double L-slot patch antenna array was presented by Chitra and Nagrajan, wherein two separate CPW feed points were used to feed the array element and with an omnidirective radiation pattern [69].

Owing to all these facts, a 1 × 2 patch antenna array is proposed in this book. The antenna is characterized with a simple feed geometry and use of the complementary split ring resonator (CSRR) in the ground plane. The design goals of the proposed antenna for human vital sign detection are that dimensions of the antenna should not be more than 4 × 4 inch², concurrent dualband operation in the 2.44 GHz and 5.25 GHz range, and a directive radiation pattern. Table 3.1 summarizes a brief review of the microstrip antenna.

3.3.1.2 Geometry

The geometry of the proposed antenna is shown in Figure 3.3. The rectangular patch is designed using the empirical relations given in [62] and a CSRR is used in the ground plane. The CSRR used in the antenna structure behaves like an electric dipole which can be excited by an axial electric field. The electrical equivalent of CSRR is an LC tank circuit [73]. The width of CSRR slot is 0.5 mm, and the gap G is equal to 0.5 mm. The radius of the outer concentric ring of CSRR is 3.5 mm and that of the inner ring is 2 mm. The length of the patch (L_P) is 32.50 mm and the width (W_P) is 33.75 mm.

A substrate of dimension ($L_S \times W_S$) 78 mm × 97 mm is used. Both L_1 and L_2 are 10 mm. A corporate feed network is designed according to the relationships reported by Munson [74]. The feed width W is kept at 3.6 mm and the subsequent width is decreased accordingly. The height of feed from the substrate boundary (L_3) is 12 mm. W and W_1 are kept at 1.8 mm and 3.6 mm, respectively. The patch is placed at a horizontal distance (W_3) of 10 mm from the substrate. On the ground plane, both CSRR are kept at an equal height, that is, $G_L = 40$ mm. GW_1 and GW_2 are kept at 41.50 mm and 36.50 mm, respectively.

3.3.1.3 Parametric Study

To consolidate the functioning of the antenna, parametric studies of the effect of patch dimensions and CSRR position are carried out. Figure 3.4 shows the

TABLE 3.1

State-of-the-Art Microstrip Antenna Array

Contribution	Operation Band(in GHz)	Feed Mechanism	Directivity	Nature of Array
Swelam et al. [66]	3.5 and 5	Separate aperture feed	Omnidirectional	1 × 2 and 1 × 4 microstrip patch elements
Khraisat et al. [67]	2.4	Microstrip line feed	Directional	1 × 4 patch elements
Ghosh and Parui [68]	5.25	Microstrip line feed	Directional	2 × 2 slotted microstrip patch
Chitra [69]	Wideband (2.4 to 3.5 and 4 to 5.4)	Two separate CPW feed	Omnidirectional	Two separate patches are used for individual band with independent feeds
Lau et al. [70]	Wideband (3.4 to 4.5)	Proximity coupled feed	Omnidirectional and Unidirectional at specific bands	U-shaped slot on the patch and antenna element is a sandwich of three dielectric layers
Li et al. [71]	2.4 to 2.5 and 5.1 to 5.9	Coaxial cable feed	Directional	A long dipole and two short dipoles
Present work	2.44 and 5.25	Corporate feed	Directional	1 × 2 patch with CSRR loading in the ground

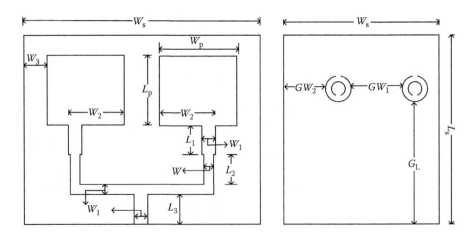

FIGURE 3.3

Geometry of a concurrent dualband directive antenna. (From Iyer, B., Pathak, N., and Ghosh, D., IEEE Asia-Pacific Conference on Applied Electromagnetics, Malaysia, pp. 150–153, 2014 [72].)

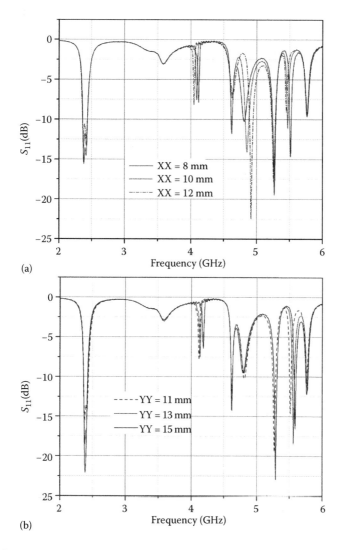

FIGURE 3.4
CSRR position parametric study: (a) XX = horizontal position with YY = 11 mm, W_p = 33.75 mm, L_p = 32.50 mm; (b) YY = vertical position with XX = 8 mm, W_p = 33.75 mm, L_p = 32.50 mm. (From Iyer, B., Pathak, N., and Ghosh, D., IEEE Asia-Pacific Conference on Applied Electromagnetics, Malaysia, pp. 150–153, 2014 [72].)

parametric study of the effect of the CSRR position while other dimensions are kept constant.

The effects of the variation of patch dimensions are also examined. The lower frequency of the microstrip patch is sensitive to the variations in the width (W_p), while the higher frequency is sensitive to the variation in length (L_p). Also, the desired frequency bands are sensitive to variation in the CSRR

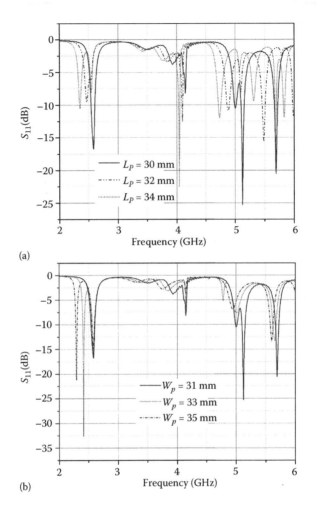

FIGURE 3.5
Patch dimension variation effect: (a) L_P = patch length with XX = 10 mm, W_P = 31 mm, YY = 12 mm; (b) W_P = patch width with XX = 10 mm, L_P = 32 mm, YY = 12 mm. (From Iyer, B., Pathak, N., and Ghosh, D., IEEE Asia-Pacific Conference on Applied Electromagnetics, Malaysia, pp. 150–153, 2014 [72].)

position. Figure 3.5 illustrates the parametric study of the patch dimensions. The simulated surface current at the desired bands is shown in Figure 3.6, which confirms the dualband nature of the proposed antenna. Figure 3.7 shows the fabricated prototype of the proposed antenna.

3.3.1.4 Experimental Characterization and Discussion

The measurement setup for the proposed antenna is shown in Figure 3.8. Figure 3.9 shows the simulated and measured return loss characteristics of

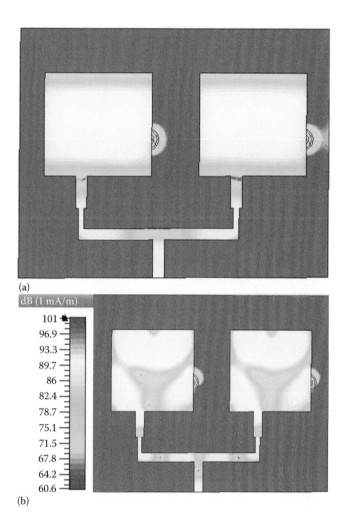

FIGURE 3.6
Surface current distribution at (a) 2.44 GHz and (b) 5.25 GHz. (From Iyer, B., Pathak, N., and Ghosh, D., IEEE Asia-Pacific Conference on Applied Electromagnetics, Malaysia, pp. 150–153, 2014 [72].)

the designed antenna prototype. The result confirms the dualband characteristics of the proposed antenna. Due to a slight deviation from the calculated parameter values and the errors during the fabrication process, some deviation is observed in the measured results. Another band is also present in simulation as well as in our measurement near 6 GHz. However, it may be neglected as the return loss is around –7 dB (maximum).

The E-plane and H-plane radiation patterns have been measured in the anechoic chamber with the transmitting antenna, and the designed prototype (receiver) was distanced at 1.5 m. Figure 3.10 depicts the anechoic

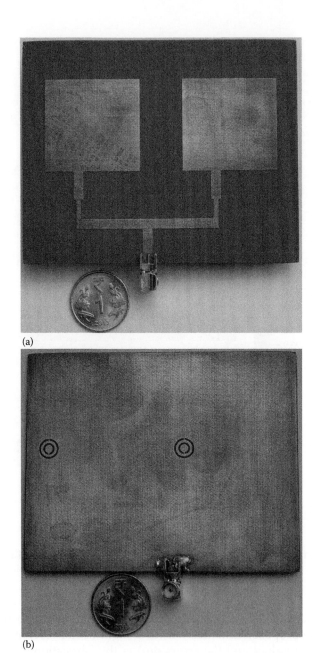

FIGURE 3.7
Fabricated antenna prototype: (a) patch side and (b) ground side with $W_P = 33.75$ mm, XX = 1 mm, $L_P = 32.5$ mm, YY = 11.5 mm, $L_S = 78$ mm, $W_S = 97$ mm, $L_1 = L_2 = 10$ mm.

FIGURE 3.8
Measurement setup for antenna characterization.

chamber measurement setup used in the characterization of the proposed antenna. Here, a wideband source operating between 10 MHz and 20 GHz (R\&S: SMR20) has been used along with a wideband reference antenna (ELMIKA: 1 GHz to 8 GHz). The source is operated at 2.44 GHz and 5.25 GHz frequencies with a 15 dBm power output.

The antenna under test (AUT) is rotated in all directions (0° to 360° with a step size of 5°) by the positioner to estimate the radiation pattern. The radiated power is measured and recorded using the power meter (R&S NRVS1020). Figure 3.11 and Figure 3.12 depict the 3D radiation patterns for the proposed antenna array. The comparisons of simulated and the measured radiation pattern are illustrated in Figure 3.13 and Figure 3.14. These plots confirm the directive radiation properties of the antenna.

Measurement of gain has been carried out by the substitution method with a standard gain horn antenna (reference antenna) working in the range of 900 MHz to 8 GHz. Table 3.2 summarizes the simulated and measured gains at 2.44 GHz and 5.25 GHz. A difference of an average 1.2 dB in the simulated and measured gains has been observed, which may be attributed to the constraints in the fabrication process and measurement errors.

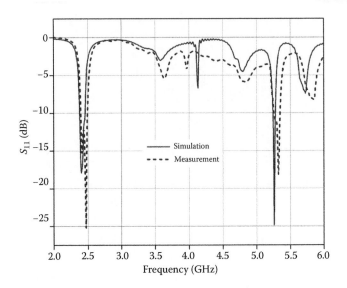

FIGURE 3.9
Return loss characterization of the directive antenna with W_p = 33.75 mm, XX = 1 mm, L_p = 32.5 mm, YY = 11.5 mm.

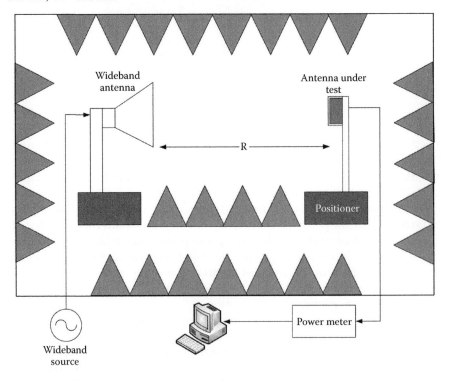

FIGURE 3.10
Typical anechoic chamber measurement setup.

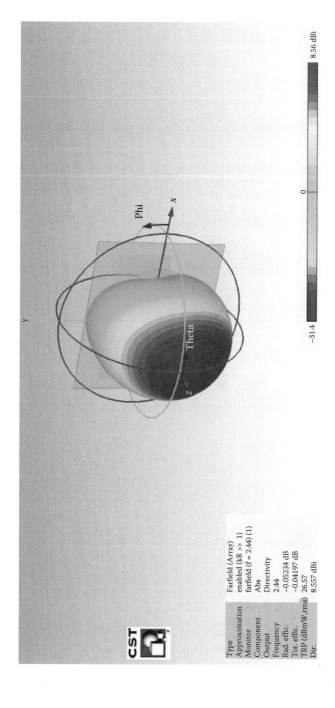

FIGURE 3.11

Three-dimensional radiation pattern at 2.44 GHz.

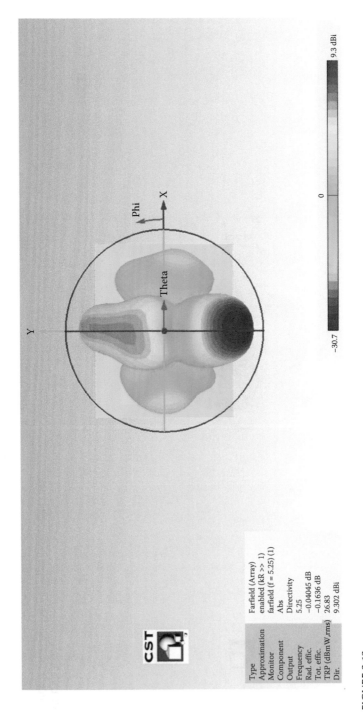

FIGURE 3.12
Three-dimensional radiation pattern at 5.25 GHz.

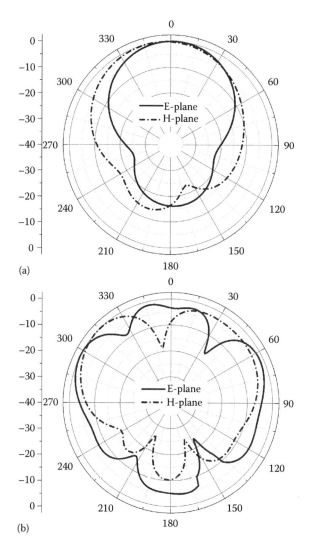

FIGURE 3.13
Simulated radiation pattern of the directive patch antenna array at (a) 2.44 GHz and (b) 5.25 GHz.

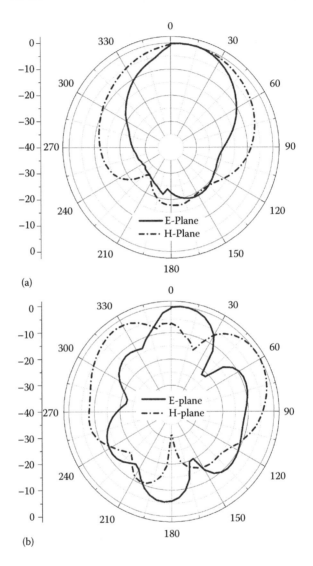

(a)

(b)

FIGURE 3.14
Measured radiation pattern of the directive patch antenna array at (a) 2.44 GHz and (b) 5.25 GHz.

TABLE 3.2

Measured Gain Characteristics

Frequency (GHz)	Simulation Gain (dBi)	Measurement Gain (dBi)
2.44	8.5	7.2
5.25	9.3	8.1

3.3.2 Omnidirectional 1 × 2 Patch Antenna Array

3.3.2.1 Geometry

A 1 × 2 monopole concurrent dualband patch antenna array also has been designed and fabricated for the NIVSD analysis. The array is a combination of two identical microstrip patches fed by a single feed line. Individual patches of the designed dualband monopole antenna consist of two rectangular elements that are piled over each other. Figure 3.15 depicts the geometry of the proposed antenna array. The smaller rectangular monopole element governs the higher frequency operation of the antenna. It has a width of 11.2 mm and a length of 7.1 mm. The larger rectangular monopole element controls the lower frequency operation of the antenna which is 15 mm in width and 18.5 mm in length. An additional rectangular monopole element is positioned exactly below the higher frequency monopole element, having a width of 6 mm and length of 5 mm along with an extra small metallic strip with width 3.5 mm and length 10 mm. This arrangement is intended to get a better return loss at both frequencies of interest. Rectangular monopole elements are printed on one side of the NH9320 substrate. The overall length and width of the substrate is 60 mm and 79 mm, respectively. The ground plane is kept on the other side of substrate with a length of 29.4 mm and a width of 79 mm. The bandwidth and operating frequency is sensitive to the ground plane dimensions. A simple corporate feed network is designed according to [74] for the proposed array antenna. It has a length of 6.3 mm and width of 38.2 mm.

3.3.2.2 Characterization

The fabricated antenna prototype is as depicted in Figure 3.16. Figure 3.17 indicates the simulated and measured return loss characteristics for the antenna. Mismatch in responses is due to limitations of the fabrication process.

The fabricated prototype shows a considerable bandwidth achievement over the desired bands of operation. Table 3.3 compares the measured performance of the fabricated antenna with reported printed monopole single patch antenna.

Figure 3.18 illustrates the 3D radiation pattern for the omnidirective patch antenna array at the two design frequencies. The simulated and the measured radiation patterns in Figure 3.19 and Figure 3.20 show the broadside directive nature of the antenna.

The radiation pattern is highly omnidirective in nature, which makes this antenna suitable for WLAN and Bluetooth applications. The radiation pattern and return loss characteristics confirm the dualband nature of this antenna. However, this kind of radiation pattern is suitable for applications in which the occupancy has to be predicted. The very reason is it may pick up signals from its surroundings is due to its broadside directivity. The detailed NIVSD-centric utility analysis of the developed antenna prototype is given in Chapter 5.

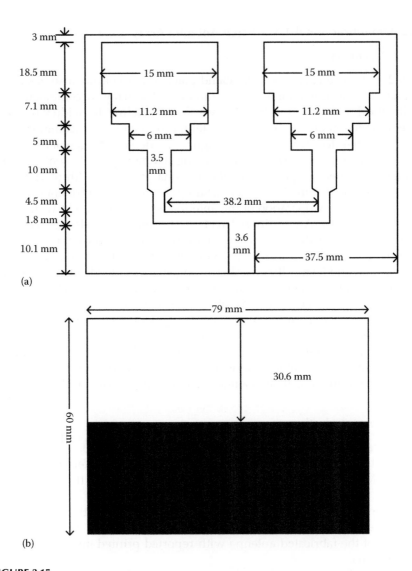

(a)

(b)

FIGURE 3.15
Geometry of the 1 × 2 dualband omnidirectional array: (a) patch side and (b) ground side. (From Iyer, B., Kumar, A., and Pathak, N. P., International Conference on Signal Processing and Communication (ICSC–2013), Noida, India, pp. 57–61, 2013 [75].)

(a)

(b)

FIGURE 3.16
Measurement prototype of the 1 × 2 dualband omnidirectional array: (a) patch side and (b) ground side.

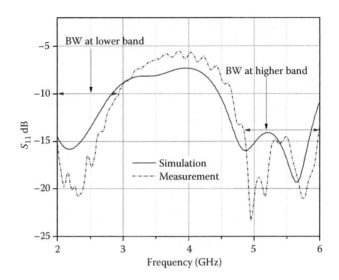

FIGURE 3.17
Return loss characterization of the 1 × 2 dualband omnidirectional antenna array.

TABLE 3.3

Bandwidth Comparison

Bandwidth at	Rathore et al. [63]	Proposed Work
2.44 GHz	760 MHz	975 MHz
5.25 GHz	720 MHz	1000 MHz

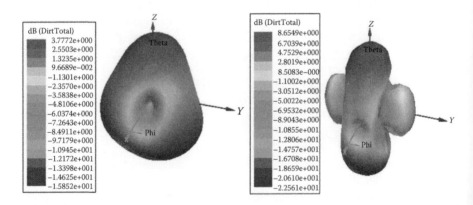

FIGURE 3.18
Three-dimensional radiation patterns for the omnidirectional antenna array at 2.44 GHz and 5.25 GHz.

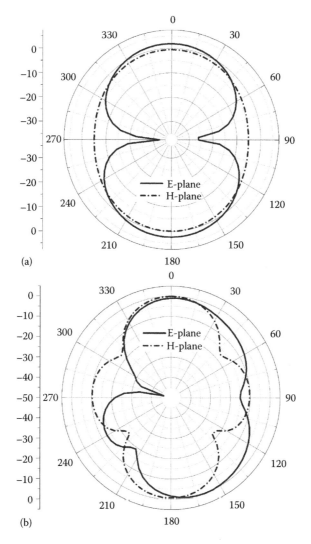

FIGURE 3.19
Simulated radiation patterns of the omnidirective patch antenna array at (a) 2.44 GHz and (b) 5.25 GHz.

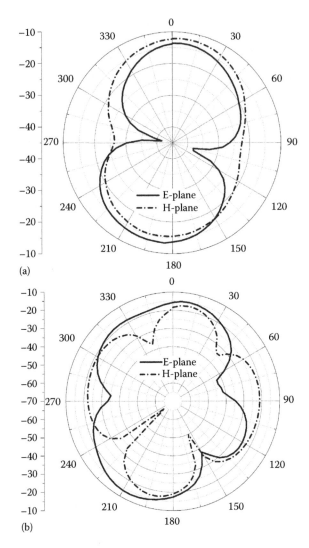

FIGURE 3.20
Measured radiation patterns of the omnidirective patch antenna array at (a) 2.44 GHz and (b) 5.25 GHz.

3.4 Conclusions

A low-cost, simple in geometry, and easily reproducible concurrent dualband patch antenna array design and characterization has been discussed in this chapter. The proposed design is carried out to fulfill the needs of the NIVSD system. Three different configurations, namely, a single patch, omnidirective array, and a directive array, have been incorporated in our design for this purpose.

4

Concurrent Dualband Front-End
Elements for NIVSD Sensors

4.1 Introduction

This chapter describes design details of the different subsystems in the proposed concurrent dualband sensor system. A concurrent dualband Wilkinson power divider (WPD) is designed as an interconnector. In a wireless receiver design, the low noise amplifier (LNA) is a critical crossing point between the antenna and baseband circuitry. As a front end of the receiver, within the bandwidth of interest, it must capture and amplify a very low power or voltage signal along with embedded random noise which the antenna feeds to it. Hence, design of a concurrent dualband LNA is carried out by using the standard hybrid monolithic integrated circuit (HMIC) technique and by using a high mobility electron transistor (HEMT). These subsystems operate simultaneously at 2.44 GHz and 5.25 GHz frequency bands and provide a compact, power-efficient, and low-cost solution due to its concurrent operation. Further, two oscillators are designed to operate at the 2.44 GHz and 5.25 GHz bands. The proposed design is simulated and verified with an advanced design system (ADS-2009). The simulated design is then fabricated on a commercial substrate (NH9320) which is a polytetrafluoroethylene (PTFE)/glass/ceramic dielectric. It has a dielectric constant ε_r = 3.2, height (h) = 1.524 mm, thickness (t) = 18μm, and a loss tangent (σ) = 0.0024. The standard wet etching technique has been used in the fabrication process. The design details and characterization are described in the following sections.

4.2 Concurrent Dualband WPD

Since its first announcement by E. J. Wilkinson, a power combiner and divider hold the key for successful implantation of various microwave/millimeter wave systems [76]. Power combiners are used to combine the power from

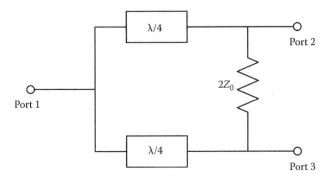

FIGURE 4.1
A basic three-port Wilkinson power divider.

several inputs whereas a power divider is necessary to distribute the input power among several outputs. In general, a power divider and combiner is a three-port network having single input and double outputs (for divider) or vice versa. The basic functionality of a power divider and combiner can be understood by its scattering parameters [77]. A simple power divider cannot fulfill the properties of lossless, reciprocity, and matching at the same time. To overcome this drawback, the WPD was developed. An isolation resistor used between the output ports helps to achieve the above desired properties in a WPD. Besides isolation, this resistor protects the output ports at the working frequencies. A WPD can be of any number of output ports. A basic three-port WPD is shown in Figure 4.1. The analysis of a WPD can be carried out by even and odd mode analysis method [77].

4.2.1 Related Work

Many efforts were made by the researchers to acquire the desired power division or combination characteristics with different architectures of the WPD. A dualband power divider design using a simplified two-section transformer was proposed by Srisathit et al. However, it suffers from poor return loss and isolation [78]. A power division technology was proposed by Wu et al. using an inductor and a capacitor connected in parallel with the isolation resistor [79]. Topologies such as a two-way broadband microstrip-matched power divider, DGS-based power divider, transmission line structure, two-section impedance transformers with a parallel RLC circuit, input stub with cascaded transmission line sections, and two central transmission line stubs with a low-pass filter to achieve wide-band operation have also been reported in the literature [80–83]. All these mechanisms have their limitations, such as the size of the circuitry, number of operational bands, and extra circuitry to achieve dualband operation. The proposed NIVSD system requires a WPD/WPC, which should be compact and must support concurrent operation at 2.44 GHz and 5.25 GHz without any additional switching mechanism. To meet these requirements, the structure reported by Cheng et al. is further modified to work with the frequency ratio of 2.15 ($f_2/f_1 = 5.25/2.44$) [82]. A key-shaped compact WPD is proposed and used in this analysis. The values of Z_A, Z_B, and Z_{OC} are estimated as a function of this frequency ratio. Equations 5.1 to 5.3 are used to estimate the required values of Z_A, Z_B, and Z_{OC}.

$$Z_A = \sqrt{2}Z_O \tan \frac{\pi}{2}\varepsilon \tag{4.1}$$

$$Z_B = \sqrt{2}Z_O \cot \frac{\pi}{2}\varepsilon \tag{4.2}$$

$$Z_{OC} = \frac{Z_O}{2} \frac{\tan^2 \pi\varepsilon}{\sqrt{2}} \tan \frac{\pi}{2}\varepsilon \tag{4.3}$$

4.2.2 Geometry

Figure 4.2 shows the schematic of the proposed concurrent dualband WPD/WPC to operate simultaneously at 2.44 GHz and 5.25 GHz. A polygon-shaped conductor is used to connect Z_A and Z_B with length of 4.2 mm at an angle of 45° with the horizontal axis. The angle between the microstrip lines of Z_A and Z_{OC} is 30°. The isolation between Port 2 and Port 3 is obtained by connecting a 100Ω resistor in between. Due to the modification in the circuit topology and the use of polygon-shaped conductors and tapers, the dimensions are further optimized to meet the frequency ratio

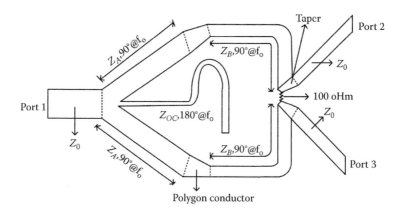

FIGURE 4.2
Geometry of the WPD. (From Iyer, B., Kumar, A., and Pathak, N. P., International Conference on Signal Processing and Communication (ICSC–2013), Noida, India, pp. 57–61, 2003 [75].)

TABLE 4.1

Geometry of WPD

	Dimensions			
	With Empirical Relations		Optimized	
Impedance (Ω)	L (mm)	W (mm)	L (mm)	W (mm)
$Z_A = 45.72$	12	4.2	12	3
$Z_B = 109.36$	12.78	0.74	12.78	0.9
$Z_{OC} = 56.44$	24.4	3	28.8	1.02

Source: Iyer, B., Kumar, A., and Pathak, N. P., International Conference on Signal Processing and Communication (ICSC–2013), Noida, India, pp. 57–61, 2003 [75].

requirement while conforming to compact size, better return, and insertion loss with isolation on both bands. Table 4.1 summarizes the dimensions of the proposed WPD. The length of open stub and Z_B are further miniaturized by meandering.

4.2.3 Characterization

Figure 4.3 shows the measurement setup and fabricated prototype of the proposed key-shaped compact WPD. The overall dimensions of the WPD are 4.2 cm × 2.5 cm. The effectiveness of WPD operation is further confirmed by its S-parameter values. Table 4.2 provides S-parameter analysis for the proposed WPD prototype.

Figure 4.4 illustrates the simulated and measured return loss, insertion loss, and isolation characteristics of the proposed WPD structure at the desired bands. It clearly indicates it is the concurrent dualband nature of operation. A WPD can act as a power divider as well as a power combiner. This capability of the proposed prototype is further verified by providing a 10 dBm power at Port 1. Here, two independent signal sources R&S SMR 20:10 MHz to 20 GHz and Agilent E8257D PSG: 100 kHz to 20 GHz are used at the two designated bands. The WPD is connected to the source via a cable and connector. The power level is measured with the help of a power meter (R&S NRVS1020). Table 4.3 provides the capacity of the proposed prototype as a power divider.

The capacity of a WPD as a concurrent power combiner is validated by providing 8.8 dBm input power at Port 2 while operating at 2.44 GHz and 8 dBm of input power at Port 3 for 5.25 GHz via cables and connectors. Variations in the supplied power at every individual ports is due to the loss incurred in cables and connectors. At Port 1, the measured power is 9.20 dBm, which indicates that the proposed WPD can also be used as a power combiner for concurrent dualband operation.

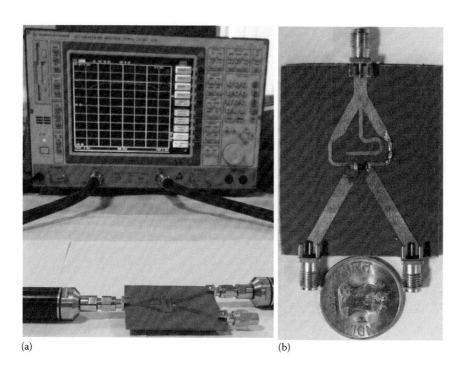

(a)   (b)

FIGURE 4.3
Characterization of the proposed concurrent dualband WPD: (a) measurement setup and (b) the fabricated prototype. (From Iyer, B., *Advances in Intelligent Systems Research*, 137, 834–846, 2017 [38].)

TABLE 4.2

S-Parameters for the Proposed WPD Prototype

Frequency (GHz)	Return Loss (S_{11} dB)		Insertion Loss (S_{21} dB)		Isolation (S_{32} dB)	
	Simulation	Measurement	Simulation	Measurement	Simulation	Measurement
2.44	−13.45	−11.84	−3.39	−3.48	−19.05	−11.44
5.25	−9.03	−8.54	−3.88	−4.35	−13.78	−18.71

TABLE 4.3

WPD as a Power Divider

Frequency (GHz)	Input Power at Port 1 (dBm)	Output Power at Port 2 (dBm)	Output Power at Port 3 (dBm)
2.44	9.02	5.83	5.94
5.25	8.06	4.30	4.45

Source: Iyer, B., *Advances in Intelligent Systems Research*, 137, 834–846, 2017 [84].

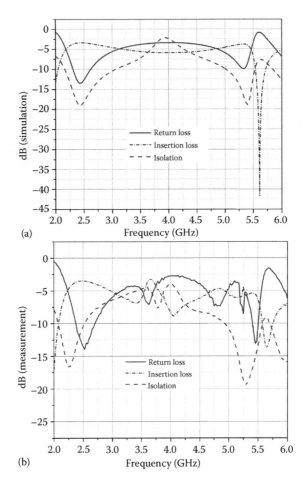

FIGURE 4.4
S-parameter analysis of the proposed concurrent dualband WPD: (a) simulation and (b) measurement. (From Iyer, B., Kumar, A., and Pathak, N. P., International Conference on Signal Processing and Communication (ICSC–2013), Noida, India, pp. 57–61, 2003 [75].)

4.3 Concurrent Dualband LNA

4.3.1 Related Work

One of the technical bottlenecks for a multistandard transceiver is the implementation of the low noise amplifier (LNA) that can operate at two distinct frequency bands. Conventional dualband architecture adopts two parallel single-band LNAs [85]. This approach suffers from high implementation cost, large chip area, and high power consumption. Efforts were initiated to comprehend a compact dualband LNA by switched mode operation. In this approach, capacitor and switched inductors are used to toggle between the desired bands [86,87]. However, this approach also suffers from additional switching circuitry and associated delays with excess chip area to provide the dualband operation. The aforementioned drawbacks may be overcome by designing an LNA with concurrent operation at the desired bands. This kind of approach is based on hardware sharing, that is, the same hardware supports simultaneous operation at the desired bands. Due to this feature, the cost, size, and power consumption of the system can be decreased considerably. A variety of approaches have been proposed to design and develop a concurrent dualband LNA. The versatility in the design is obtained by choosing a specific set of operating frequencies, a good fabrication technology, and an appropriate matching network. Table 4.4 gives a brief overview of LNA design.

For the proposed system design, a concurrent dualband LNA is designed, measured, and fabricated to operate at 2.44 GHz and 5.25 GHz band. A single pseudomorphic HEMT (p-HEMT) viz. ATF-36163 is used as an active device. The proposed LNA is comprehended using a standard HMIC process with a major focus on maximum hardware sharing without any lumped circuitry. The conceptual diagram of the dualband LNA is shown in Figure 4.5. The entire design procedure in ADS consists of the following major steps:

- DC bias simulation and bias network design
- S-parameter analysis
- Design of matching network
- Simulation and optimization of the layout using electromagnetic design system (EMDS)
- Fabrication

TABLE 4.4

State-of-the-Art for a Multiband LNA

Contribution	Technology	Frequency Band	Matching Network	Gain(Av)	NF(dB)	Return Loss(dB)
Dao et al. [85][a]	0.18 µm CMOS	2.4 and 5.2 GHz	Using discrete component	11.8 and 16	3.6 and 2.5	−16 and −30
S.Yoo and H.Yoo [86]	0.18 µm CMOS	2.3 to 2.5 GHz and 5.1 to 5.9 GHz	Switched inductor & capacitor	15 and 15	2.3 and 2.4	−25 and −20
Martins et al. [87][a]	0.35µm CMOS	0.9 GHz and 1.8 GHz	With discrete component	−	3 and 3	−10 and −10
Hashemi and Hajimiri [88]	0.35µm CMOS	2.45 and 5.25 GHz concurrent	With discrete component	14 and 15.5	2.3 and 4.5	−25 and −15
Proposed Approach	p-HEMT	2.44 and 5.25 GHz concurrent	Microstrip matching network	7.15 and 7.80	4.3 and 4.6	−10.54 and −15.98

[a] Simulation results are reported.

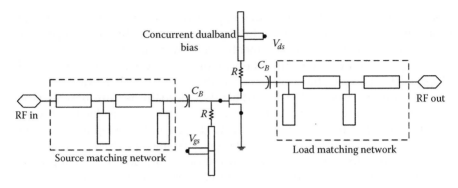

FIGURE 4.5
Geometry of the concurrent dualband LNA for NIVSD. (From Iyer, B., and Pathak, N. P., *Microwave and Optical Technology Letters*, 56, 2, 391–394, 2014 [89].)

4.3.2 DC Bias Point and Stability Analysis

DC bias simulation is performed using the ADS model for ATF-36163 transistor. From the FET Curve Tracer template, an operating quiescent point is selected for linear operation of the transistor in the active region. The DC bias point selected from the simulation setup is given in Table 4.5.

In stability analysis, it is found that ATF-36163 is unconditionally stable at 5.25 GHz, but is not at 2.44 GHz. Thus, it needs to be stabilized before its use. A stabilizing resistance of a suitable value may be appended either at the input or at output end of the transistor. Furthermore, this resistance may be connected either in series or in parallel. In general, appending a single stabilizing resistor at either end of a transistor stabilizes it. A shunt stabilizing resistance R_d is added at the output end of ATF-36163 in order to stabilize it for LNA design. From the load stability circle of the transistor, it can be stabilized at 2.44 GHz (and above) by using a stabilizing resistance greater than 17.95Ω. The required minimum value approaches 100Ω as the operating frequency tends toward 1 GHz. To ensure unconditional stability up to the lowest RF of 1 GHz, a stabilizing shunt resistance of 100Ω is selected for connection at the output end of the DC biased ATF-36163. S-parameters for the transistor at the specified bias are obtained using S-parameter simulation in ADS, using the transistor's model. Initially, a DC feed (ideal) is used in the

TABLE 4.5

Bias Point of ATF 36163 BLKG Transistor

Parameter	Parameter	Value
V_{ds}	Operational Drain to Source Voltage	2.75 Volts
I_{ds}	Operational Drain to Source Current	13 mA
V_{gs}	Operational Gate to Source Voltage	−0.2 Volts

TABLE 4.6

S-Parameters of ATF 36163 BLKG Transistor

Frequency	S(1,1)	S(1,2)	S(2,1)	S(2,2)
2.44 GHz	0.84∠–52.01°	0.03∠41.17°	3.17∠118.2°	0.63∠–12.60°
5.25 GHz	0.57∠–108.24°	0.05∠–3.85°	2.47∠58.33°	0.49∠–10.04°

TABLE 4.7

Stability Analysis of ATF 36163 BLKG Transistor

Frequency	Δ	K	μ	μ_{prime}
2.44 GHz	0.61	1.25	1.20	1.05
5.25 GHz	0.41	2.25	1.72	1.50

bias network for isolation of RF. The S-parameter obtained from the simulation is given in Table 4.6.

The transistor stability is analyzed at the two design frequencies with the help of K-Δ and μ test. Basic equations for stability measurement is given as [90]

$$|\Delta| = |S_{11}S_{22} - S_{12}S_{21}| < 1 \tag{4.4}$$

$$K = \frac{1 - |S_{11}|^2 - |S_{22}|^2 + |\Delta|^2}{2|S_{12}S_{21}|} > 1 \tag{4.5}$$

$$\mu = \frac{1 - |S_{11}|^2}{|S_{22} - \Delta S_{11}^*| + |S_{12}S_{21}|} > 1 \tag{4.6}$$

$$\mu_{PRIME} = \frac{1 - |S_{22}|^2}{|S_{11} - \Delta S_{22}^*| + |S_{12}S_{21}|} > 1 \tag{4.7}$$

Δ, K, μ, and μ_{prime} values from Table 4.7 signify that the transistor is unconditionally stable at both the frequencies of interest. Further, DC feed in the bias network is replaced by a novel concurrent dualband DC bias network design.

4.3.3 Design of Concurrent DC Bias Network

In general, a microstrip transmission line (TL)–based DC bias tee network consists of a quarter-wave impedance transformer with high-characteristic impedance. Such networks work at the designed frequency and its odd harmonics. However, it is not useful in a multiband circuit where high input impedance is required at multiple uncorrelated frequencies. Hence, a concurrent dualband DC bias network is proposed which is realized using microstrip TL sections only. Figure 4.6 shows the DC bias network.

A DC bias voltage source is applied to a TL section TL_1 with characteristic impedance Z_1 and electrical length $\theta_1(f)$. TL_1 is connected in shunt at the middle of another TL section TL_2 with characteristic impedance Z_2 and electrical length $2\,\theta_2(f)$. One end of TL_2 is left open while its other end is connected to the main RF signal-carrying TL path. The structure is designed in such a way that it exhibits high input impedance Z_{IN} at the two RF frequencies of interest f_1 and f_2. As one end of TL_2 is open, Z_{IN} will be high at frequencies where TL_2 is the total electrical length is an integer multiple of 180°.

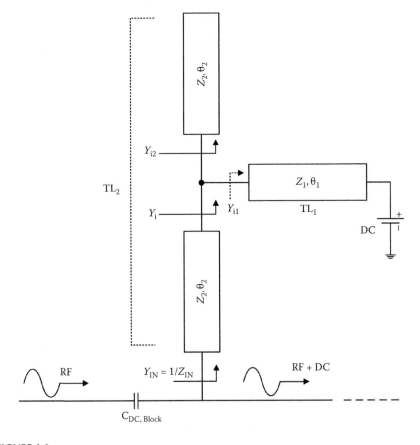

FIGURE 4.6
Geometry of the concurrent dualband DC bias network. (From Iyer, B., and Pathak, N. P., *Microwave and Optical Technology Letters*, 56, 2, 391–394, 2014 [89].)

For short TL length, the electrical length of TL_2 is kept equal to 180° at the higher operating frequency f_2. In other words,

$$\theta_{(f)} = \left[\frac{\pi}{2} \cdot \frac{f}{f_2} \right]$$ (4.8)

Connecting TL_1 in shunt, exactly in the middle of this TL_2, will not affect the high Z_{IN} value at f_2. The DC bias voltage source is applied through another end of TL_1. Design parameters of TL_1 are calculated by considering the requirement that Z_{IN} is high at the lower operating frequency f_1 also. The input admittance at half of the first open ended TL_2 sections are

$$Y_{i2}(f) = j \frac{\tan \theta_2(f)}{Z_2} = j Y_2 \tan \left[\frac{2}{\pi} \cdot \frac{f}{f_2} \right]$$ (4.9)

During RF analysis, the DC connection is considered as analog ground. Therefore, the input admittance of the AC grounded TL_1 is given as

$$Y_{i1}(f) = j \frac{1}{jZ_1 \tan \theta_1(f)} = j Y_1 \cot \theta_1(f)$$ (4.10)

Overall admittance seen at the edge of the second half of TL_2 is given as

$$Y_i(f) = Y_{i1}(f) + Y_{i2}(f) = j \left[(Y_2 \tan \theta_2(f)) - (Y_1 \cot \theta_1(f)) \right]$$ (4.11)

The final input admittance shown by the entire structure at any frequency is then calculated as

$$Y_{IN}(f) = Y_2 \frac{Y_i(f) + j Y_2 \tan \theta_2(f)}{Y_2 + j Y_i(f) \tan \theta_2(f)}$$ (4.12)

With $Z_{IN}(f_1) = \infty$ or, equivalently, $Y_{IN}(f_1) = 0$, the numerator is required to be zero. Thus

$$Y_i(f_1) + j Y_2 \tan \theta_2(f_1) = j \left[(2 Y_2 \tan \theta_2(f_1)) \cdot (Y_1 \cot \theta_1(f_1)) \right] = 0$$ (4.13)

$$\Rightarrow \theta_1(f_1) = \tan^{-1} \left[\frac{Z_2}{2 Z_1 \tan \theta_2(f_1)} \right] = \tan^{-1} \left[\frac{Z_2}{2 Z_1 \tan \left(\frac{\pi}{2} \cdot \frac{f_1}{f_2} \right)} \right]$$ (4.14)

Equation 4.8 and Equation 4.14 indicate that the characteristic impedances of both the TL sections can be chosen arbitrarily ensuring fabrication feasibility. With the aforementioned design relations, the proposed DC bias network will exhibit high input impedance at any two uncorrelated desired frequencies f_1 and f_2. Here, f_1 and f_2 are 2.44 GHz and 5.25 GHz, respectively. S-parameters and corresponding stability measures are unaffected by the introduction of this bias network and are the same as that with a DC feed (ideal). Furthermore, the electromagnetic simulation using EMDS shows that the proposed dualband DC bias network offers very high input impedance. Figure 4.7 shows the EMDS response of the proposed DC bias network.

A high characteristic impedance value, within feasible fabrication limits, is chosen for all TL sections in the bias network, which further increases the input impedance at the two RF frequencies. For instance, in the current scenario, widths of all TL sections are kept at 1 mm, leading to high characteristic impedance. Table 4.8 tabulates dimensions of the proposed concurrent dualband DC bias network for ideal and EMDS simulations.

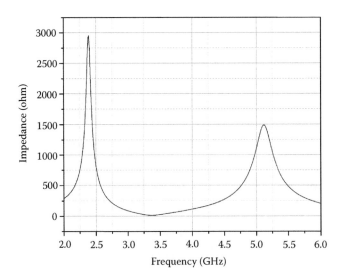

FIGURE 4.7

EMDS response of the concurrent dualband DC bias network.

TABLE 4.8

Dimensions of the Concurrent Dualband Bias Network

Frequency	Simulation	Width (mm)	Length (mm)
2.44 GHz	Ideal	1	6.52538
5.25 GHz			9.2569
2.44 GHz	EMDS	1	6.46
5.25 GHz			9.26

4.3.4 Concurrent Dualband Matching Network

The dualband matching network is designed using microstrip lines by calculating the reflection coefficients at the source and load ends of the transistor with the proposed DC bias network. The matching network employs series TL sections and stubs to transfer complex impedance seen at the terminals of the transistor to 50Ω at the port. Two stubs are connected in shunt to the main line and are open circuited.

Figure 4.8 shows the impedance transformer structure that is used for dualband matching. The problem of infeasible characteristic impedances is mitigated by considering four physical lengths of series TL sections and stubs as design parameters. Hence, a designer can arbitrarily set characteristic impedances of all TL sections. Such consideration not only allow the dualband matching of unequal complex impedances, but also admits feasible fabrication of microstrip transmission-line sections.

Consider the network shown in Figure 4.8. Let Y_L be the load admittance which is converted to Y_B by the first series TL section of length L_2 and an open circuit shunt stub of length S_2. This admittance is further transformed into standard admittance Y_0 by another series TL section of length L_1 and an open ended shunt stub of length S_1. For ease of analysis and feasible fabrication, characteristic impedance of all TL sections and stubs are set to standard 50Ω. Considering the normalized admittance with respect to Y_0 as y_L, y_B, and y_A the transmission line theory leads to the following design relations.

$$y_B = \left[\frac{(y_L + j\tan\beta L_2)}{1 + jy_L \tan\beta L_2} + j\tan\beta S_2 \right] \tag{4.15}$$

$$y_A = \left[\frac{(y_B + j\tan\beta L_1)}{1 + jy_B \tan\beta L_1} + j\tan\beta S_1 \right] \tag{4.16}$$

$$y_L = g_L + j\beta_L \tag{4.17}$$

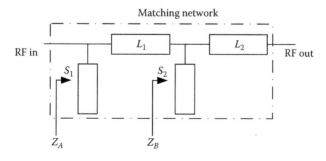

FIGURE 4.8
Concurrent dualband matching network.

Further, consider the two frequencies of interest as f_1 and f_2. Consequently, two different load admittances YL_1 and YL_2 need to be matched at the two frequencies f_1 and f_2 respectively. Moreover, the propagation constant (γ) also varies with the operating frequency. Accordingly, six equations are obtained for simultaneous impedance matching at the two design frequencies. Given the values for y_{L1} and y_{L2} the lengths L_1, L_2, S_1, and S_2 are adjusted such that all these equations are satisfied simultaneously, that is, load impedances at f_1 and f_2 are simultaneously matched to 50Ω.

Based on the derived equations, a MATLAB® program is developed to provide all possible solutions for feasible length parameters for dualband impedance matching. Table 4.9 lists the required reflection coefficients at both ends of the biased transistor at the two frequencies of interest. Required impedances can be calculated from the reflection coefficient values. Considering the complex impedances as target load, design parameters for the input and the output matching networks are obtained using the MATLAB program. The code is written to solve the design Equations 4.15 to 4.17 for concurrent dualband complex impedance matching through the conventional double open-ended shunt stub structure. Inputs to the program are the two design frequencies along with the corresponding source and load refection coefficients. Moreover, substrate parameters, such as dielectric constant, height, and so on, are also provided in order to consider their effects while performing computations at the two frequencies of interest. The program provides all possible solutions in terms of physical lengths of the series, TL sections and the open circuited shunt stubs. Based on the reflection coefficients, corresponding electrical lengths and physical lengths of the matching networks are given in Table 4.10.

Physical lengths, obtained from ADS *Line Calc tool*, are used for creation of layout. These dimensions are further optimized using EMDS simulation to obtain the desired results. Table 4.11 gives these optimized dimensions for the matching network. A layout is created, including the input and the output matching networks, with the help of the physical lengths that are obtained from ideal simulation in ADS. Ports are placed at the input and the output of the network, as well as at every point where an external lumped device interfaces with the network. The matching network in an ADS circuit is then replaced with this layout and EMDS cosimulations are performed.

While designing the layout, the widths of all microstrip lines are kept constant at 3.64 mm, which corresponds to the characteristic impedance 50Ω of the chosen substrate. In addition, a 50Ω microstrip line and a taper are used

TABLE 4.9

Reflection Coefficients

Frequency	At Source (Γ_s)	At Load (Γ_L)
2.44 GHz	$-0.70 + j0.66$	$-0.18 - j0.11$
5.25 GHz	$-0.92 - j0.26$	$-2.1 \times 10^{-3} - j0.39$

TABLE 4.10

Electrical and Physical Length of the Matching Network

Matching Network	L_1 (mm)		L_2 (mm)		S_1 (mm)		S_2 (mm)	
	Electrical (degree)	Physical (mm)	Electrical (degree)	Physical (mm)	Electrical (degree)	Physical (mm)	Electrical (degree)	Physical (mm)
Input	63.1920	13.44	59.0322	12.55	55.562	11.81	67.0168	14.25
Output	91.5162	19.46	140.5461	29.89	53.4102	11.36	22.5687	4.80

TABLE 4.11

Optimized Dimensions of the Matching Network

Matching Network	L_1 (mm)	L_2 (mm)	S_1 (mm)	S_2 (mm)
Input	6.73	41.44	14.91	13.88
Output	5.88	12.37	13.3	15.82

Source: Iyer, B., and Pathak, N. P., *Microwave and Optical Technology Letters*, 56, 2, 391–394, 2014 [89].

at both ends of the matching network. It helps to mitigate the effect of evanescent modes caused due to junctions, transitions, and port connections.

4.3.5 Measurement and Analysis

Figure 4.9 depicts the measurement setup and the fabricated prototype of the proposed concurrent dualband LNA. For analysis purposes, S-parameters are calculated from the measurement setup. Figure 4.10 provides the plot of the measured and simulated S_{11} and S_{21} and is summarized in Table 4.12.

The noise figure (NF) is measured with the help of an Agilent noise figure meter setup. Figure 4.11 shows the measurement setup and the plot of simulation and measured NF of the proposed concurrent dualband LNA and is summarized in Table 4.13. The proposed concurrent dualband LNA

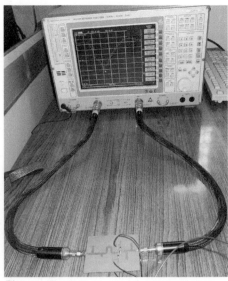

(a)   (b)

FIGURE 4.9

Characterization of the proposed concurrent LNA: (a) the fabricated prototype and (b) measurement setup. (From Iyer, B., Kumar, A., Pathak, N. P., and Ghosh, D., International Microwave and Radio Frequency Conference (IMaRC–2013), New Delhi, India, pp. 1–4, 2003 [92].)

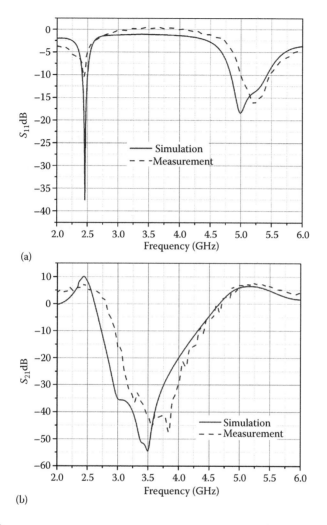

FIGURE 4.10
S-parameter performance of the concurrent dualband LNA: (a) S_{11} and (b) S_{21}. (From Iyer, B., and Pathak, N. P., *Microwave and Optical Technology Letters*, 56, 2, 391–394, 2014 [89].)

TABLE 4.12

Gain Analysis of the Dualband LNA

Frequency (GHz)	S(1,1) dB		S(2,1) dB	
	Simulation (EMDS)	Measured	Simulation (EMDS)	Measured
2.44	−17.24	−10.54	10.11	7.16
5.25	−13.48	−15.98	6.39	7.80

Source: Iyer, B., and Pathak, N. P., *Microwave and Optical Technology Letters*, 56, 2, 391–394, 2014 [89].

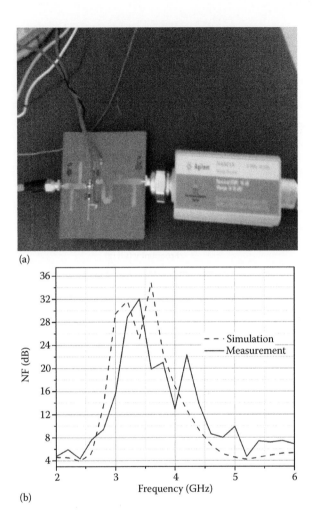

(a)

(b)

FIGURE 4.11
Noise figure analysis of the concurrent dualband LNA: (a) measurement setup and (b) simulation and measurement performance. (From Iyer, B., and Pathak, N. P., *Microwave and Optical Technology Letters*, 56, 2, 391–394, 2014 [89].)

TABLE 4.13

NF Analysis

Frequency (GHz)	NF(dB)	
	EMDS Simulation	**Measured**
2.44	3.9	4.3
5.25	4.2	4.6

exhibits NF at par with LNAs reported in [88,91]. Hence, the amplifier passes the preferred frequencies while rejecting the undesired frequencies with a reasonable NF. All the aforementioned characteristics make the proposed concurrent dualband LNA suitable to be used as a subsystem in an RF sensor system for NIVSD.

4.4 Oscillators

To cater to the need of a source, two oscillators are designed to operate at 2.44 GHz and 5.25 GHz. A microwave oscillator consists of frequency selective circuit (resonator), negative resistance cell (transistor with positive feedback and biasing circuit), and output matching circuit as shown in Figure 4.12. The Barkhausen criterion for sustainable oscillation states that

- Amplitude condition: The cascaded gain and loss through the amplifier/feedback network must be greater than unity.
- Phase condition: The frequency of oscillation will be at the point where the loop phase shift totals 360 (or zero) degrees.

Figure 4.13 indicates the basic equivalent circuit for an oscillator. The input impedance is current (or voltage) dependent as well as frequency dependent and can be written as

$$Z_{in}(V,\omega) = R_{in}(V,\omega) + jX_{in}(V,\omega) \tag{4.18}$$

The device is terminated with passive load impedance Z_L, defined as

$$Z_L(\omega) = R_L(\omega) + jX_L(\omega) \tag{4.19}$$

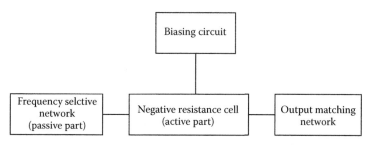

FIGURE 4.12
Block diagram of negative resistance-based typical oscillator.

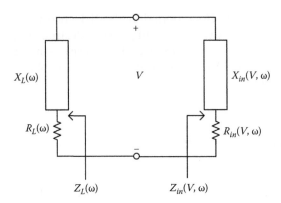

FIGURE 4.13
Equivalent circuit for one-port negative resistance microwave oscillators.

Applying Kirchhoff's voltage law (KVL), we get

$$Z_{in}(V,\omega) + Z_L(\omega) = 0 \tag{4.20}$$

The one port network is stable if

$$\text{Re}\left[Z_{in}(V,\omega) + Z_L(\omega)\right] > 0 \tag{4.21}$$

For oscillation, negative resistance of the active device in a series circuit must exceed the load resistance by about 20 percent (i.e., $R_{in} = -1.2R_L$):

$$R_{in}(V,\omega) + R_L(\omega) = 0 \tag{4.22}$$

$$X_{in}(V,\omega) + X_L(\omega) = 0 \tag{4.23}$$

Initially, it is necessary for the overall circuit to be unstable at a certain frequency (i.e., sum of R_L and R_{in} be a negative number):

$$\left|R_{in}(V,w)\right| > R_L(\omega) \tag{4.24}$$

Any transient excitation or noise then causes the oscillation to build up at a frequency ω. The load is passive, $R_L > 0$ and Equation 4.22 indicates that $R_{in} < 0$. Thus, a positive resistance implies energy dissipation; a negative resistance implies an energy source. The condition of Equation 4.24 controls the frequency of oscillation. For the stability of an oscillator, high-Q resonant circuits such as cavities and dielectric resonators are used.

The design procedure described here is general and applies to any transistor circuit configuration as long as its S-parameters are known. Unlike the amplifier circuit, the transistor for an oscillator design must be unstable. In a transistor oscillator, a negative resistance is effectively created by terminating a potentially unstable transistor with impedance designed to drive the device in an unstable region. Figure 4.14 depicts the block diagram of a transistor-based oscillator. The following section describes the design procedure of an oscillator.

4.4.1 DC Bias Simulation and Bias Network Design

A Si-doped AlGaAs FET NE4210S01 is selected for this design since its operating frequency is from 2 GHz to 18 GHz. DC bias simulation is performed in ADS-2009 using the transistor model. DC bias point for oscillator design was selected as $V_{DS} = 2V$ and $I_{DS} = 10$ mA and $V_{GS} = 0.69$ V. A microstrip line biasing circuitry is selected for the DC biasing of the transistor. Figure 4.15 shows a microstrip line bias network.

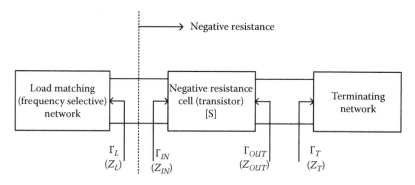

FIGURE 4.14
Block diagram of microwave transistor-based oscillator.

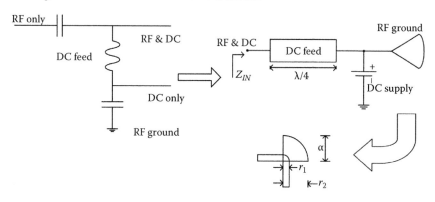

FIGURE 4.15
A microstrip line bias network. (From Iyer, B., *Advances in Intelligent Systems Research*, 137, 834–846, 2017 [84].)

TABLE 4.14

Geometry of the Bias Network

Z_0 (Ω)	Frequency (GHz)	W (mm)	L (mm)
130	2.44	0.43	20.39
	5.25	0.43	9.44

Source: Iyer, B., *Advances in Intelligent Systems Research,* 137, 834–846, 2017 [84].

TABLE 4.15

Dimensions of the Radial Stub

Frequency (GHz)	r_1 (mm)	α (degree)	r_2 (mm)
2.44	0.43	60	12.89
5.25	0.43	60	6.86

Source: Iyer, B., *Advances in Intelligent Systems Research,* 137, 834–846, 2017 [84].

In microstrip implementation, the inductor may be substituted by a high impedance line and the capacitor can be realized as an open or a radial stub. A radial stub is used to provide a broadly resonant RF short circuit. When cascaded with high-impedance quarter wavelength transmission lines, the radial stub provides an effective decoupling network for microwave amplifiers and other active components [93]. The high impedance (selected as 130Ω) quarter wavelength (with electrical length 90°) microstrip line is followed by a radial stub. The dimensions are calculated using *Line Calc tool* in ADS 2009. The bias network design is similar for the 2.44 GHz and 5.25 GHz bands, except for the variation in the dimensions. Table 4.14 and Table 4.15 provide the dimensions of the bias network.

4.4.2 Stability Analysis and S-Parameter Simulations

S-parameter simulation is performed with the DC bias network. Table 4.16 provides the S-parameters for the proposed oscillator design. Using S-parameters, transistor stability is analyzed at the two design frequencies with the help of K-Δ and μ tests as per Equations 4.4 to 4.7. Table 4.17 summarizes the stability analysis for the proposed oscillators. It is observed that the transistor is unconditionally unstable at the desired frequencies.

TABLE 4.16

S-Parameters of NE4210S01 Transistor

Frequency	S(1,1)	S(1,2)	S(2,1)	S(2,2)
2.44 GHz	1.208∠−8.20°	0.075∠83.81°	2.311∠−128.84°	1.110∠−14.79°
5.25 GHz	1.960∠−48.89°	0.256∠50.71°	6.814∠168.06°	1.490∠−54.86°

Source: Iyer, B., *Advances in Intelligent Systems Research,* 137, 834–846, 2017 [84].

TABLE 4.17

Stability Analysis of NE4210S01 Transistor

Frequency	Δ	K	μ	μ_prime
2.44 GHz	1.18	−0.84	−0.92	−0.77
5.25 GHz	1.86	−0.45	−0.65	−0.36

Source: Iyer, B., *Advances in Intelligent Systems Research*, 137, 834–846, 2017 [84].

4.4.3 Design of Matching Networks

Based on S-parameters, an impedance-matching network design is initiated. It can be designed either analytically or with the Smith chart as a graphical design tool. For the common source with series capacitive feedback S-parameters, the input and the output stability circles are drawn on the Smith chart using the Smith chart utility in ADS-2009, as shown in Figures 4.16 and 4.17. The input stability circle is a contour in the source plane that indicates source termination values that makes the output reflection coefficient to have unity magnitude. An output reflection coefficient less than unity indicates a stable device, while an output reflection coefficient greater than unity indicates a potentially unstable device.

As seen from Figures 4.16 and 4.17, a great deal of flexibility is available in the selection of the reflection coefficient for the input matching network.

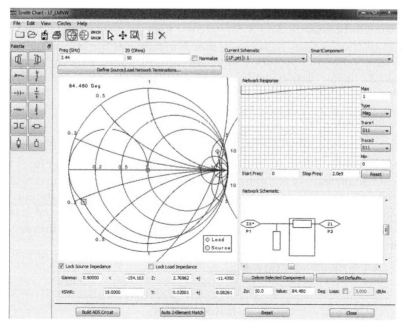

FIGURE 4.16
Matching network design using Smith chart utility in ADS for 2.44 GHz.

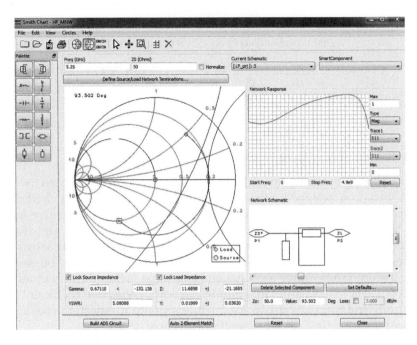

FIGURE 4.17
Matching network design using Smith chart utility in ADS for 5.25 GHz.

Theoretically, any Γ_S residing inside of the stability circle should satisfy our requirements because S_{11} and S_{22} are greater than unity. In practice, however, one has to choose Γ_S in such a way that it maximizes the output reflection coefficient. Values of reflection coefficients are calculated in such a way that they satisfy the oscillation condition. Table 4.18 provides the calculated value of reflection coefficients.

$$\Gamma_L = \frac{1}{\Gamma_{OUT}} ; \Gamma_{OUT} = S_{22} \tag{4.25}$$

The conversion of the electrical parameters of the transmission lines into physical dimensions is accomplished using the *Line Calc tool* in ADS-2009. The dimensions of the TLs are computed for a NH9320 substrate and are summarized in Table 4.19. A 50Ω microstrip of 5 mm in length and a taper of 1.5 mm in length are connected to the output port side to minimize the fringing field effect.

TABLE 4.18

The Reflection Coefficients

Frequency (GHz)	Γ_L
2.44	0.90∠14.79
5.25	0.67∠54.86

TABLE 4.19

Dimensions of the Matching Network

Frequency (GHz)	Z_O	Effect	Electrical Length	Width (mm)	Length (mm)	Optimized Length(mm)
2.44	50Ω	Inductive	84.48°	3.64	18.05	10.12
		Capacitive	103.61°		22.05	21.38
5.25		Inductive	93.50°	3.68	9.16	5.92
		Capacitive	118.92°		11.66	15

Source: Iyer, B., *Advances in Intelligent Systems Research*, 137, 834–846, 2017 [84].

4.4.4 Design of Resonator Network

As the oscillator design uses the small signal S-parameters and Z_{IN} becomes less negative with the buildup of oscillator output, it is necessary to choose Z_L so that $Z_L + Z_{IN} < 0$. Otherwise, the oscillations will cease when the increasing power increases Z_{IN} to a point where $Z_L + Z_{IN} > 0$. In general, a value of Z_L is chosen such that

$$Z_L = \frac{-Z_{IN}}{3}; \ X_L = -X_{IN} \tag{4.26}$$

The resonators are realized by using open stub *TL* and estimated on the basis of

$$\theta = \tan^{-1}\frac{X_S}{Z_O} + 90 \quad \text{for positive reactive part} \tag{4.27}$$

$$\theta = \tan^{-1}\frac{X_S}{Z_O} \quad \text{for negative reactive part} \tag{4.28}$$

The reactive part of Z_L is chosen to resonate the circuit. Table 4.20 summarizes the details of the resonator design.

TABLE 4.20

Summary of the Resonator Design

Parameter	At 2.44 GHz	At 5.25 GHz
Z_{IN} Ω	$-43.91 - j260.9$	$-23.29 - j107.94$
Z_L Ω	$14.63 + j260.9$	$7.76 + j107.94$
Electrical length	169.15°	155.14°
Physical length (mm)	36	15.65
Physical width (mm)	3.64	3.68
Optimized length (mm)	33	9

Source: Iyer, B., *Advances in Intelligent Systems Research*, 137, 834–846, 2017 [84].

4.4.5 Harmonic Balance Simulation

The next step is to perform a harmonic balance simulation to predict oscillator characteristics, that is, the output power spectrum and phase noise performance at both the frequencies. *OscPort* is an ADS probe component that is used to calculate the oscillator waveform using a harmonic balance simulation. It calculates the large signal steady state form of the oscillatory signal. The resulting frequency spectrum and corresponding phase noise are shown in Figures 4.18, 4.19, and 4.20.

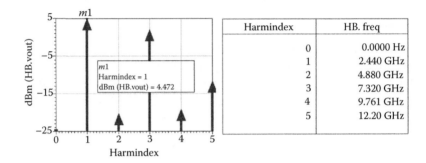

FIGURE 4.18
Oscillator performance at 2.44 GHz simulation.

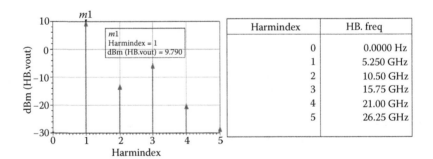

FIGURE 4.19
Oscillator performance at 5.25 GHz simulation.

4.4.6 Measurement Results

Based on the analysis from Sections 4.4.1 to 4.4.5, a fabricated prototype of the proposed oscillators is devised. Further, measurement of these oscillators is carried out with Agilent Filedfox Spectrum Analyzer (100 MHz to 6 GHz). Figure 4.21 depicts the measurement setup. The fabricated prototypes of the proposed oscillators are shown in Figures 4.22 and 4.23. The measured power spectrum of the oscillators is depicted in Figure 4.24.

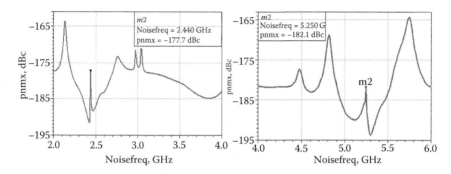

FIGURE 4.20
Simulated phase noise performance of the oscillator.

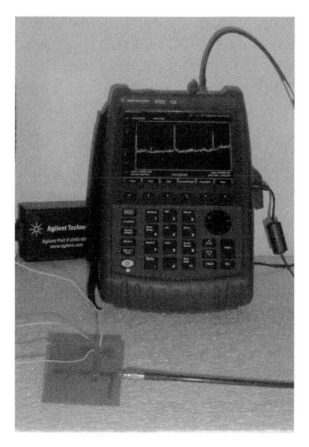

FIGURE 4.21
The oscillator measurement setup. (From Iyer, B., *Advances in Intelligent Systems Research*, 137, 834–846, 2017 [84].)

FIGURE 4.22
Fabricated prototype for 2.44 GHz band. (From Iyer, B., *Advances in Intelligent Systems Research*, 137, 834–846, 2017 [84].)

FIGURE 4.23
Fabricated prototype for 5.25 GHz band. (From Iyer, B., *Advances in Intelligent Systems Research*, 137, 834–846, 2017 [84].)

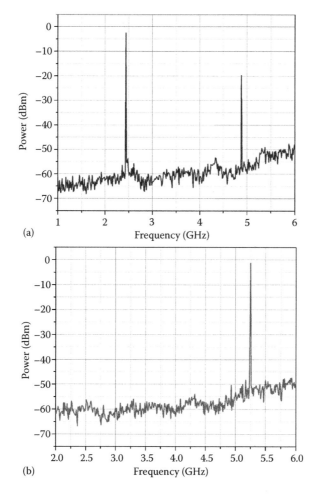

FIGURE 4.24
Measured power spectrum at (a) 2.44 GHz and (b) 5.25 GHz. (From Iyer, B., *Advances in Intelligent Systems Research*, 137, 834–846, 2017 [84].)

The phase noise of the oscillators had been calculated using the relation [94]

$$P_{NOISE} = P_{SB} - P_C - 10\log_{10}(RBW)dBc \qquad (4.29)$$

where P_{SB} = sideband power in dB at an offset of 100 KHz, P_C = carrier power in dB, and RBW = resolution bandwidth of the spectrum analyzer in MHz. Considering the losses incurred due to the measurement setup and tolerance of the fabrication process, the carrier power is assumed to be 0 dBm along with a RBW of 200 MHz. Table 4.21 summarizes the simulated and measured phase noise of the oscillators at 2.44 GHz and 5.25 GHz.

TABLE 4.21

Phase Noise Analysis

Frequency (GHz)	P_{SB} dB	Phase noise (dBc)	
		Simulation	Measurement
2.44	−46	−177.7	−109
5.25	−43	−182.1	−106

Source: Iyer, B., *Advances in Intelligent Systems Research*, 137, 834–846, 2017 [84].

4.5 Conclusions

This part of the book describes the design of a concurrent dualband WPD that operates simultaneously at 2.44 GHz and 5.25 GHz. The aim is to have a compact low-loss circuit as WPD, which is a critical element in the front-end design as an interconnector. Further, a concurrent dualband LNA is designed to operate at 2.44 GHz and 5.25 GHz. The design is incorporated with a standard HMIC technique and using ATF-36163, a p-HEMT active device. Measured performance of the fabricated LNA exhibits the required dualband response with a wideband rejection in between the desired band. A 2.44 GHz and 5.25 GHz oscillator is also designed to have a compact source for the proposed NIVSD sensor to be handheld.

5

Characterization of a Concurrent Dualband NIVSD Sensor

5.1 Introduction

This chapter presents details of experimental validation of the proposed concept. In this direction, the proposed concept is first verified using a VNA as a transceiver element. Then, the measurement setup is operated simultaneously at the designated operational bands. Finally, a PCB is devised from indigenously comprehended concurrent dualband components and commercial ICs such as SMD GaLi-24+ power amplifier (PA) and SMD SYH 63LH+ mixer. The baseband signal processing is carried out to extract the desired signal. The block diagram of the proposed non-invasive vital sign detection sensor is shown in Figure 5.1.

The proposed sensor works on the Doppler principle. It transmits 2.44 GHz and 5.25 GHz carrier signals simultaneously directed toward the human subject under test. The received signals consist of the additional information of human chest disarticulation modulated onto the carrier. The desired information of the human respiration and heartbeats can then be obtained from the baseband signal via proper signal processing.

5.2 Design Considerations

To design a successful NIVSD sensor system, criteria such as transmitted power, null point consideration, radar range, and safety factors must be taken into account.

5.2.1 Safety Factor (S)

Since the proposed sensor is used in the detection of human vital signs using RF signals, in many applications it is necessary to ensure that the RF exposure is within a safe limit. Excessive RF exposure may be hazardous to the

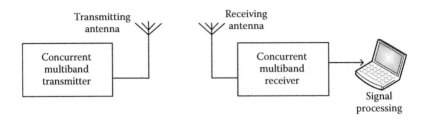

FIGURE 5.1
Block schematic of proposed NIVSD sensor.

human being. According to the IEEE RF safety standards, at the designated operational bands of the proposed system, maximum EM radiation density levels up to 10 W/m² are considered safe [95]. The safety factor (S) is estimated as

$$S\left(\frac{W}{m^2}\right) = \left[\frac{P_T G_T}{4\pi L^2}\right]$$ (5.1)

where P_T = radiating power in dBm, G_T = antenna gain in dBi, and L = distance between the antenna and the human subject in meters.

5.2.2 Transmitted Power

The proposed system may be employed for human vital sign detection for continuous and longer duration, such as patient monitoring in hospitals, and for shorter duration in applications, such as identifying life under debris. In the first case, the use of PA is not advised because it is the most power-consuming element, whereas for such applications, the power level must be as low as possible. In the second case, the detection sensitivity is the primary goal. Moreover, the monitoring and detection process is carried out for a shorter duration. Hence, use of a power amplifier will be beneficial in such applications. In addition, the EM radiation must satisfy the safety considerations narrated in Section 5.2.1.

5.2.3 Optimum and Null Point Consideration

Direct conversion architecture is adopted to realize the proposed system. It is often adopted in the Doppler radar detection system due to its simple architecture with single tone transmission and one-step conversion [1,2,43–45]. As discussed in Section 1.2.2.3, the null point problem may severely degrade the detection reliability at high frequencies in a single-band system used for vital sign sensor application. With concurrent dualband operation, it is guaranteed that an optimal point in the detection process always exists for at least one band. Further, the effect of null point detection can be minimized by incorporating reconfigurability or in-band tunability to select an optimum frequency ratio for the detection process (see Section 5.3).

5.2.4 Radar Range Equation

In radar operations, the detection range of radar is related to the transmitter, receiver, antenna, the operational environment, and the target characteristics. This is also the best tool to understand and study the factors affecting the performance of the system. The radar range equation is given as

$$P_R = P_T\left[A\frac{G_T G_R}{4\pi}\left(\frac{\lambda}{4\pi R^2}\right)\right] \tag{5.2}$$

where P_T is the transmitted power (dB), A is the radar cross section area (in m^2), and λ is the wavelength of the signal to be transmitted (in m). G_T and G_R are the gains of the transmitter and receiving antenna (in dBi). From this equation, one can easily infer that for long range of transmission, the transmitted power should be large and the antenna must be highly directive.

5.2.5 Receiver Noise Figure

For cascaded subsystem stages of the receiver, the overall noise figure (NF) is calculated by the Friis equation and is given as

$$NF = 1 + (NF_1 - 1) + \frac{NF_2 - 1}{A_1} + \frac{NF_3 - 1}{A_1 A_2} \tag{5.3}$$

Here, A_1 and A_2 are the gains of two stages, and NF_1 and NF_2 are the noise figures of the subsequent stage.

5.2.6 Link Budget

Link budget calculation is an effective cost function that provides the ability of the system to detect signals over a distance. For estimation of the link budget over a particular distance, free space path loss ($FSPL$) plays a pivotal role and is estimated as

$$FSPL = 20\log_{10}\left[\frac{4\pi L}{\lambda}\right] \tag{5.4}$$

where L is the distance from the transmitter (in meters) and λ *(c/f)* is the wavelength of the signal. Based on the *FSPL*, the link budget or link sensitivity is estimated as

$$P_{RX} = P_{TX} + G_{TX} - L_{TX} - L_{FS} + G_{RX} - L_{RX} \tag{5.5}$$

where P_{TX} = transmitted output power in dBm, G_{TX} = transmitter antenna gain in dBi, L_{TX} = transmitter losses in dB, L_{FS} = free space losses in dB, G_{RX} = receiver antenna gain in dBi, and L_{RX} = receiver losses in dB.

5.2.7 Link Budget

It is the minimum signal level within the acceptable signal-to-noise ratio *(SNR)* that can be detected by the system:

$$R_S = -174\,\text{dBm/Hz} + NF + 10\log_{10}(B) + SNR \tag{5.6}$$

where NF is the noise figure obtained in Equation 5.3 and B is the system bandwidth.

5.3 Measurement System

To validate the proposed concurrent dualband NIVSD, an ADS simulation has been carried out using the measured S-parameters of the subsystems and standard ADS library components. Figure 5.2 shows the simulation setup to decide the validity of the proposed concept.

Here, the human being under test is modeled with the RESP and HB signals and two-phase modulators, operating at 2.44 GHz and 5.25 GHz. The RESP and HB signals are obtained by the standard available source with ADS and were kept at 0.33 Hz and 1.2 Hz, respectively. Individual RF sources have been used from the ADS library. Figure 5.3 shows the received signals at individual bands along with the standard human vital sign signal. From Figure 5.3, it is clear that though the detection is carried out at different bands, the position of the desired signal peak does not change due to concurrent multiband operation. This is the significant advantage of the proposed system. Hence, without varying the measurement conditions, the advantages of lower- and higher-band operation can be achieved.

Following the simulation validation, an initial measurement has been carried out using a VNA and two concurrent dualband microstrip patch antennas in a noisy environment. Agilent Fieldfox RF Analyzer (N9912A: 2 MHz – 6 GHz) has been used as a transceiver element. Figure 5.4a shows the initial measurement setup using a VNA. The human subject is positioned at a distance of 1 m away

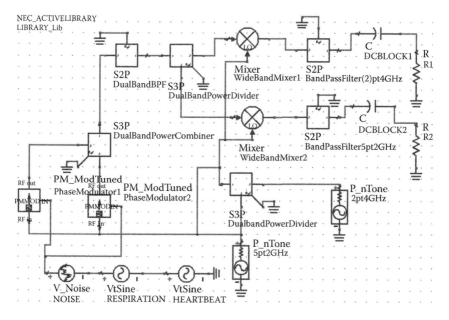

FIGURE 5.2
ADS simulation for proposed NIVSD sensor. (From Iyer, B., Garg, M., Pathak, N. P., and Ghosh, D., *Proceedings of International Conference of Information and Communication Technologies* (ICT–2013), Tamilnadu, India, pp. 563–567, 2013 [96].)

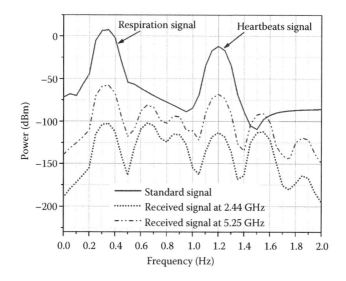

FIGURE 5.3
ADS simulation result.

from the antennas. The two antennas are distanced 17 cm apart. The samples are taken for 52 seconds from a human subject with a normal physique. Real-time readings of heartbeat and respiration rates from the VNA are captured and processed using a MATLAB® program. The sampling frequency is kept at 3.2 Hz since the maximum frequency of heartbeat is generally 1.5 Hz.

The phase information in forward transfer gain S_{21} is captured from the VNA (Figure 5.4b). The phase variation frequencies can be interpreted as the heartbeat and respiration rate. FFT and WT are applied on these signals to detect the desired frequency components of the heartbeat and the respiration rate.

Figures 5.5a,b and 5.6a,b show the FFT and WT spectrum, respectively, for the desired signal. It is observed that at lower frequency, that is, at 2.44 GHz, the noise aspect is less but at the cost of detection sensitivity. On the other hand, at higher frequency, that is, at 5.25 GHz, the detection sensitivity is increased but with the tag of noise.

From Figures 5.5 and 5.6, it is clear that even though the measurement is carried out at different bands, the detected respiration and heartbeat signals are not distorted. This is because the measurements are carried out concurrently at two bands. The resultant FFT spectrum shows that the desired signals are present along with their harmonics and noise components. Furthermore, many frequency components lie in the allowable heartbeat range. This may be because the third- and the fourth-order harmonics of the respiration signal overlap with the heartbeat signal. Here it is impossible to sense the exact heartbeat signal. This difficulty may be overcome by applying the correlation between the signals obtained from the two bands. With WT, it is easier to detect the human vital signs. Figure 5.7a,b shows the correlation spectrum for FFT and WT signals.

After application of correlation between the individual band signals, it is seen that the estimation of the desired signals can be carried out effectively. FFT-correlated spectrum shows that the respiration rate is 15 beats per minute, and the heartbeats are at the rate of 61 beats per minute.

The ambiguity in heartbeat detection from individual FFT and WT spectra is visibly eliminated in the correlated spectrum. In the single-band RF systems, switching is required to extract the advantage of multiband operations. Due to this, some delay is incorporated between the two consecutive measurements.

It is the normal tendency for heartbeats and the respiration rate of a human being to change over time. Hence, it is possible that inconsistent respiration rates and heartbeat signals are obtained after correlating the signals obtained from the switched mode operation. However, the measurements carried out by our proposed concurrent dualband setup have shown a uniform detection of signals at both the bands. This is the significant advantage of a concurrent dualband RF system over the existing single-band systems for vital sign detection. Additionally, the individual subsystems can be customized to operate at dualband concurrently via hardware sharing. This will minimize the hardware requirements as compared to the parallel mode of multiband operation.

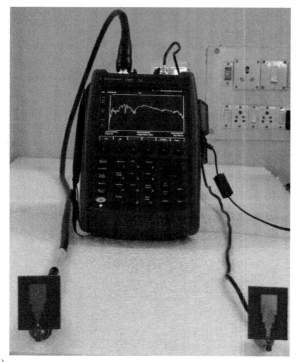

(a)

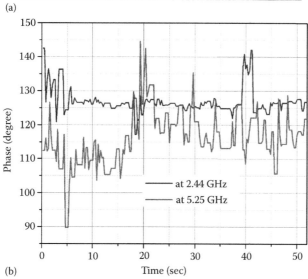

(b)

FIGURE 5.4
Characterization of the proposed concept: (a) VNA measurement setup; (b) measured phase variation information. (From Iyer, B., Garg, M., Pathak, N. P., Ghosh, D., *Elsevier Procedia Engineering*, 64, 185–194, 2013 [97].)

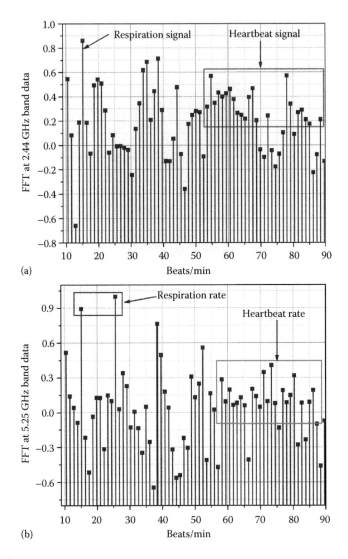

FIGURE 5.5
FFT spectrum of respiration and heartbeats at (a) 2.44 GHz and (b) 5.25 GHz. (From Iyer, B., Garg, M., Pathak, N. P., Ghosh, D., *Elsevier Procedia Engineering*, 64, 185–194, 2013 [97].)

With these initial confirmations, a more comprehensive measurement setup has been devised for the further analysis. The setup was made up of using indigenously developed dualband subsystem to operate at 2.44 GHz and 5.25 GHz band and with little laboratory equipment. Figure 5.8 shows the conceptual diagram of the proposed system.

The measurement setup shown in Figure 5.9 consists of the laboratory equipment and custom-designed dualband subsystems. Here, two RF sources (R\&S SMR20:10 MHz to 20 GHz) are used to provide the required RF signal

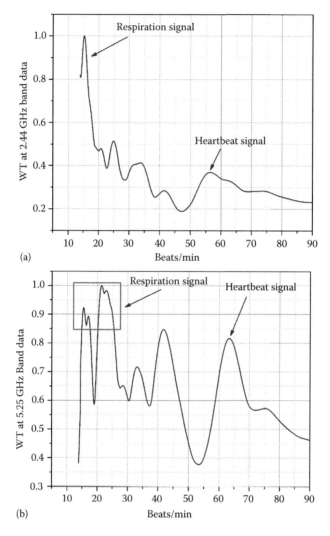

(a)

(b)

FIGURE 5.6
WT spectrum of respiration and heartbeats at (a) 2.44 GHz and (b) 5.25 GHz. (From Iyer, B., Garg, M., Pathak, N. P., Ghosh, D., *Elsevier Procedia Engineering*, 64, 185–194, 2013 [97].)

in the transmitter section. The power level is kept at 10 dBm. A dualband signal is fed to the transmitting antenna with the help of the fabricated dualband Wilkinson power combiner/divider (WPD) [75]. The measured result shows that it introduces an approximate insertion loss of −3.4 dB and −3.8 dB at 2.44 GHz and 5.25 GHz band, respectively. Note that two identical dualband patch antennas are used for transmission and reception purposes.

Further, on the receiver side, a 2.44 GHz and 5.25 GHz concurrent dualband LNA is used to boost the received signal level [89]. For the purpose of down conversion, two single-band mixers from mini circuits have been used to

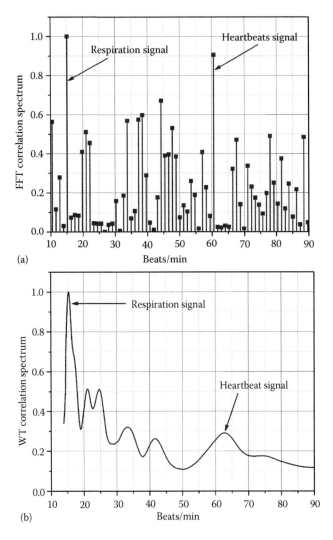

FIGURE 5.7
Correlation spectrum for human vital sign detection: (a) FFT and (b) WT. (From Iyer, B., Garg, M., Pathak, N. P., Ghosh, D., *Elsevier Procedia Engineering*, 64, 185–194, 2013 [97].)

operate at individual bands. ZEM-4300MH mixer is used at 2.44 GHz. It has 8.5 dB conversion loss and a 13 dBm power level. For 5.25 GHz, a ZMX-7GR mixer with 8.5 dB conversion loss and a 17 dBm power level has been used. The individual mixers have been fed with the local oscillator frequencies, that is, 2.44 GHz and 5.25 GHz, to obtain the baseband signal. This baseband signal has been applied to the data acquisition (DAQ) system. An IoTECH DAQ-54 system has been used with a sampling rate of 37 Hz for digitizing the baseband signal. The digitized baseband signal has been further processed

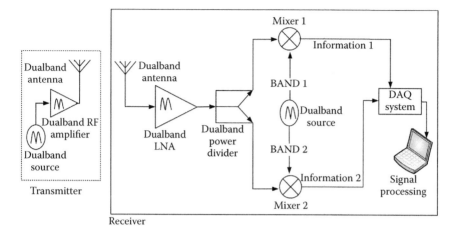

FIGURE 5.8
Conceptual diagram of proposed NIVSD sensor. (From Iyer, B., Kumar, A., Pathak, N. P., and Ghosh, D., International Microwave and Radio Frequency Conference (IMaRC–2013), New Delhi, India, pp. 1–4, 2013 [92].)

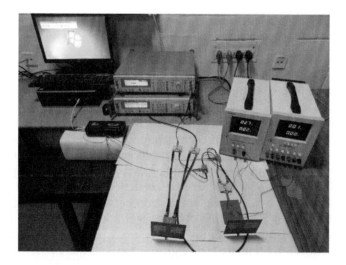

FIGURE 5.9
Measurement setup for NIVSD sensor using indigenous and laboratory equipment. (From Iyer, B., Kumar, A., Pathak, N. P., and Ghosh, D., International Microwave and Radio Frequency Conference (IMaRC–2013), New Delhi, India, pp. 1–4, 2013 [92].)

using MATLAB® to retrieve the required knowledge about the heartbeat and respiration signals. The losses due to cables and connectors have an average value of 6.55 dBm and 5 dBm at the transmitter and receiver, respectively.

The samples are taken for 120 seconds at the aforementioned sampling rate. The observations are carried out on a human being with normal health.

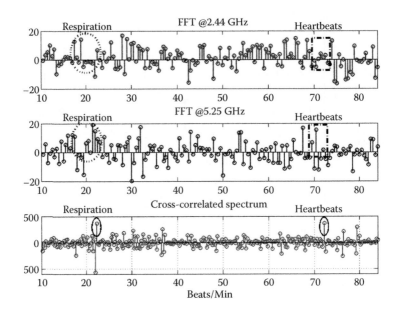

FIGURE 5.10
FFT spectrum from measurement setup at 1 m distance. (From Iyer, B., Kumar, A., Pathak, N. P., and Ghosh, D., International Microwave and Radio Frequency Conference (IMaRC–2013), New Delhi, India, pp. 1–4, 2013 [92].)

The human subject is positioned at a distance of 1 m (Figure 5.10) from the transceiver.

It is evidenced from Figure 5.10 that after FFT of the desired band signals, multiple peaks are found to be present around 20 Hz and 70 Hz. These peaks are due to noise and environmental interference. Hence, it becomes difficult to identify the exact respiration and heartbeat signals using a particular single band and may lead to the incorrect detection of human life. This ambiguity is outweighed by applying correlation between the two signals. The cross-correlation plot clearly predicts the respiration and heartbeat signals. The signals at 22 Hz and 72 Hz are the required respiration and heartbeat signals. It is also apparent that, though the measurements are carried out at different bands, the detection sensitivity is not altered. This is due to the concurrent multiband operation. In addition, the correlated signal is more sensitive in comparison with the individual bands and provides better accuracy. When the distance between the human subject and the transceiver is increased, the detection sensitivity decreases. This is due to reduced received power strength. In the current measurement setup, the PA and intermediate frequency amplifier (IFA) were not used. The detection sensitivity can be easily improved by employing a PA at the transmitter end and an IFA at the receiver end. With increased detection sensitivity, it is possible to detect life even under metal structures or other impediments.

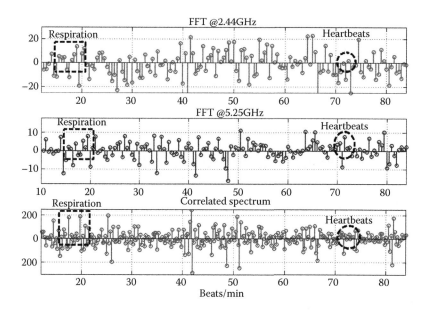

FIGURE 5.11
FFT spectrum for NIVSD using an omnidirective concurrent dualband patch antenna array at 1 m distance. (From Iyer, B., Pathak, N., and Ghosh, D., IEEE Asia-Pacific Conference on Applied Electromagnetics, Malaysia, pp. 150–153, 2014 [72].)

Further, the detection of human respiration and a heartbeat signal was also carried out by an omnidirectional patch antenna array, as described in Section 3.2.2. Figure 5.11 shows the FFT spectrum for NIVSD, using an omni-directive concurrent dualband patch antenna array, with a human subject at a distance of 0.5 m from the measurement setup.

Comparing Figures 5.10 and 5.11, it is confirmed that the noise content in the detected signal is more when a broadside directive antenna configuration is used. Hence, in order to improve the detection range and sensitivity, a directive antenna with high gain is recommended.

The performance of the proposed measurement setup may be analyzed by the link budget as a cost function. The power levels have been measured by using a power meter (R&S NRVS1020) at each stage of the setup. Table 5.1 summarizes the power levels measured at the different stages of the RF system. From the empirical relations, it is estimated that the minimum free space loss at the center frequency is 44.2 dBm.

From Equation 5.6, the link budget analysis of the measurement setup is equal to 25.7 dBm. The safety factor (S) related to EM radiation for the proposed RF system may be estimated with the help of Equation 5.1. For the measurement setup it is estimated as 87μW/m^2. The estimated electro-magnetic radiation (EMR) value is much lower than the maximum density level provided by IEEE Standards (10W/m^2) [97]. With this analysis, our own

TABLE 5.1

Measured Output Power Level

Frequency (GHz)	At WPD (dBm)	At Transmitter Antenna (dBm)	At Receiver Antenna (dBm)
2.44	5.18	5.5	−25.5
5.25	3.42		

Source: Iyer, B., Kumar, A., Pathak, N. P., and Ghosh, D., International Microwave and Radio Frequency Conference (IMaRC–2013), New Delhi, India, pp. 1–4, 2013 [92].

customized PCB for the proposed sensor had been fabricated and further analyzed in the following sections.

The selection of the proper frequency ratio plays a key role for the accuracy and sensitivity of a concurrent multiband RF system employed for NIVSD.

The performance of such concurrent multiband RF systems can be further improved by incorporating the concept of reconfigurability. It is advantageous in selecting an optimum frequency ratio for minimum EMR, which is essential for the safety of human subjects under test as well as the operator of the instrument. This novelty can be achieved by designing the individual reconfigurable subsystems. The proper selection of the frequency ratio provides a twofold advantage over the static multiband RF radios. First, the noise performance and sensitivity can be improved; second, the improved accuracy can be obtained in the detection of tiny human vital sign signals. The problem of null point detection can also be eliminated by selection of an optimal frequency ratio for the specific application. These features can be obtained via multiband RF systems with the incorporation of a varactor diode as a tuning element. By controlling the bias voltage of the varactor

TABLE 5.2

Effect of Reconfigurability

Sample No.	Band 1 (GHz)	Band 2 (GHz)	T_x Power (dBm)	R_x Power (dBm)	EMR (mW/m²)
1	2.4	5.15	11.90	−42.54	35.66
2	2.4	5.25	12.36	−43.91	39.63
3	2.4	5.35	12.90	−31.62	44.85
4	2.44	5.15	11.62	−37.20	33.40
5	2.44	5.25	12.15	−32.70	37.68
6	2.44	5.35	12.71	−30.75	42.95
7	2.48	5.15	11.34	−36.10	31.33
8	2.48	5.25	11.85	−36.50	35.23
9	2.48	5.35	12.41	−29.15	40.80

Source: Iyer, B., Pathak, N., and Ghosh, D., 2014 IEEE Region 10 Humanitarian Technology Conference (R10 HTC), Chennai, India, pp. 112–119, 2014 [21].

diode desired, tuning can be achieved. To study the effect of reconfigurability, the output power at various stages is measured with the help of a power meter (R&S NRVS1020). Table 5.2 provides the measured performance of the effect of frequency reconfigurability. It clearly shows that the performance can be improved by the reconfigurable operation as the user can decide the best frequency ratio in terms of transmitted power or EMR for a particular situation or operation.

5.4 Sensor Characterization as an Integrated System

The proposed sensor is further validated on a single substrate with relative dielectric constant of 3.2 and height of 60 mil with a loss tangent of 0.0024 with substrate height of 18 μm. The sensor is made up of indigenously fabricated concurrent dualband subsystems and some commercial components and laboratory equipment. Table 5.3 summarizes the classification of the subsystems used in the proposed sensor. Figure 5.12 shows the fabricated prototype of the proposed concurrent dualband RF sensor for NIVSD application.

TABLE 5.3

Subsystems of the Proposed System

Sr.	Subsystem	Manufacturer	Specification
1.	Source I & II	Indigenously designed	Operating at 2.44GHz and 5.25GHz
2.	Power Amplifier (Gali-24+)	Mini Circuit	Operating from DC-6GHz.
3.	WPD/WPC	Indigenously designed	Concurrent dualband 2.44 and 5.25-GHz operation.
4.	Antenna	Indigenously designed	Concurrent dualband 2.44 and 5.25-GHz operation with directive radiation pattern.
5.	LNA	Indigenously designed	Concurrent dualband operation 2.44 and 5.25-GHz
6.	Mixer I & II	Mini Circuit	IF response from DC to 1000MHz
7.	DAQ	IoTech	22 bit resolution, I/P voltage= -10VDC to 20VDC.

Source: Iyer, B., *Advances in Intelligent Systems Research*, 137, 834-846, 2017 [84].

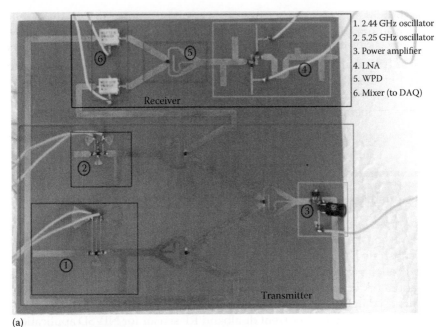

1. 2.44 GHz oscillator
2. 5.25 GHz oscillator
3. Power amplifier
4. LNA
5. WPD
6. Mixer (to DAQ)

(a)

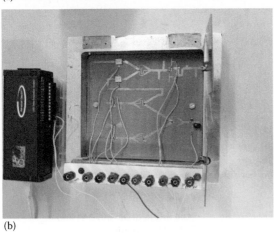

(b)

FIGURE 5.12
Characterization of the proposed concept: (a) fabricated PCB; (b) prototype with casing. (From Iyer, B., *Advances in Intelligent Systems Research*, 137, 834–846, 2017 [84].)

5.4.1   Link Budget Calculation

The measurements were carried out in indoor conditions with the distance between the antenna and the human subject varying between 0.5 m and 3 m. The experiment is carried out with three different antenna configurations such as concurrent dualband with a single patch, omnidirectional

TABLE 5.4

Link Budget Performance of the Proposed Sensor

Parameter		Antenna Array (Directive)	Antenna Array (Omnidirective)	Single Patch
Antenna Gain (dBi)		7.5	5.5	2.3
Transmitter losses (dBm)			10.41	
Receiver losses (dBm)			8.81	
Path Loss (dBm)	At 0.5 m		44.13	
	At 1 m		50.15	
	At 2 m		56.17	
	At 3 m		59.70	
Link Budget (dBm)	At 0.5 m	−38.35	−42.35	−49.05
	At 1 m	−44.37	−48.37	−55.07
	At 2 m	−50.39	−54.39	−61.09
	At 3 m	−53.92	−57.92	−64.62

Source: Iyer, B., Pathak, N. P., and Ghosh, D., *IEEE Sensor Journal*, 15, 7, 3959–3966, 2015 [98].

patch antenna array, and a direction patch antenna array. The transmitter and receiver losses are estimated by considering the contribution of individual subsystem, in terms of its gain or NF, in the system. Table 5.4 gives the detailed parametric analysis data in each of this case.

5.4.2 Link Margin Calculation

To ensure proper working of the proposed NIVSD, its sensitivity analysis is very important. Figure 5.13 shows the block diagram of the RF section of the proposed NIVSD system for sensitivity analysis. The diagram depicts the individual subsystems' gain and NF contribution. With this measurement setup, it is observed that as the distance between the transceiver and the human subject under test increases, the signal strength at the receiver end decreases considerably. The sensitivity analysis is carried out for a bandwidth of 3 Hz. The maximum heart rate varies significantly with the age which is given by [99]

$$HR_{MAX} = 205.8 - (0.685 \times \text{age}) \tag{5.7}$$

A 33-year-old male subject with normal physique has been kept under test. According to Equation 5.7, the HR_{MAX} is 183 BPM, which is approximately 3 Hz. Table 5.5 provides the performance of the proposed system under different measurement conditions.

With an output SNR value as high as 20 dB, detection of a very weak human vital sign is guaranteed. The link margin of the proposed system attains a minimum value of 74 dB with the help of a single patch antenna. This indicates that the proposed NIVSD can detect the human target accurately at considerable distance if the required link budget is less than 74 dB.

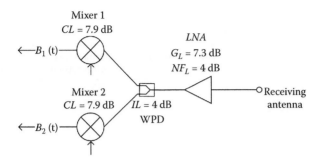

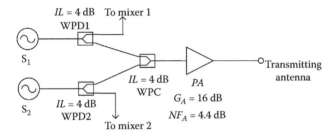

FIGURE 5.13

Block diagram of RF sensor for sensitivity analysis. (From Iyer, B., Pathak, N. P., and Ghosh, D., *IEEE Sensor Journal*, 15, 7, 3959–3966, 2015 [98].)

TABLE 5.5

Sensitivity Analysis of the Proposed Sensor

Parameter		Antenna Array (Directive)	Antenna Array (Omnidirective)	Single Patch
Thermal Noise			−174 dBm/Hz	
SNR			20 dB	
Sensitivity			−138.62 dBm	
Received Power (dBm)	At 0.5 m	−38.35	−42.35	−49.05
	At 1 m	−44.37	−48.37	−55.07
	At 2 m	−50.39	−54.39	−61.09
	At 3 m	−53.92	−57.92	−64.62
Link Margin (dBm)	At 0.5 m	100.27	96.27	89.57
	At 1 m	94.25	90.25	83.55
	At 2 m	88.23	84.23	77.53
	At 3 m	84.70	80.70	74

Source: Iyer, B., Pathak, N. P., and Ghosh, D., *IEEE Sensor Journal*, 15, 7, 3959–3966, 2015 [98].

5.4.3 Detection Range Analysis

The range of detection for this RF occupancy sensor is estimated with the help of the radar range equation as given in Equation 5.2. Here, $P_T = 10$ dB, $\lambda = 0.078$ m, and the radar cross section (σ) = 0.01 [100]. The range is estimated with different antenna configurations. Substituting the gain (G) values in Equation 5.2, the maximum distance of detection under free space condition and without any obstacle was calculated. Table 5.6 summarizes the detection range for the proposed sensor. The range may be further increased by using high gain antenna and LNA in the design architecture.

5.4.4 Safety Factor Analysis

From Equation 5.1, the level of electromagnetic radiation (EMR) to which the human subject under test was exposed during the measurements with this sensor may be estimated. Table 5.7 summarizes the safety factor analysis with different types of antenna. It is evident from the values tabulated in Table 5.7 that this sensor is safe enough to be used for the detection of human vital signs since the amount of EMR is quite small and will never turn out to be hazardous to the human subject under test.

TABLE 5.6

Detection Range of the Proposed Sensor

Antenna Configuration	Gain (dBi)	Detection Range (m)
Concurrent Dualband Single Patch	2.3	2.8
Concurrent Dualband Omnidirectional Array	5.5	4
Concurrent Dualband Directional Array	7.5	5

Source: Iyer, B., Pathak, N. P., and Ghosh, D., *IEEE Sensor Journal*, 15, 7, 3959–3966, 2015 [98].

TABLE 5.7

EMR (W/m²) Analysis

Distance (Lm)	Antenna Configuration		
	Concurrent Dualband Single Patch	Concurrent Dualband Omnidirective Patch	Concurrent Dualband Directive Patch
0.5	$1.78 \times 10{-}5$	$1.11 \times 10{-}5$	$5.41 \times 10{-}6$
1	$4.45 \times 10{-}6$	$2.78 \times 10{-}6$	$1.35 \times 10{-}6$
2	$1.11 \times 10{-}6$	$6.95 \times 10{-}7$	$3.37 \times 10{-}7$
3	$4.49 \times 10{-}7$	$3.08 \times 10{-}7$	$1.5 \times 10{-}7$

Source: Iyer, B., Pathak, N. P., and Ghosh, D., *IEEE Sensor Journal*, 15, 7, 3959–3966, 2015 [98].

5.5   Signal Processing

The performance efficiency of the baseband signal processing is the key to the success of an NIVSD system. As discussed in Section 1.2.2.5, many approaches had been reported in the literature and applied for the baseband signal processing. For the proposed NIVSD sensor, an algorithm for baseband signal processing is developed that is capable of retrieving the heartbeat and respiration rate accurately, even in a noisy environment. Figure 5.14 shows the flow chart for the proposed algorithm. The simple FFT-based signal-processing method will no longer be useful when long distance measurement is carried out. The main constraint in the signal processing is the presence of enormous noise. Among the desired signals, respiration signal is strong when compared to the heartbeat.

The extraction of heartbeat is very important, as it is weak in comparison to the respiration signal. Hence, special care needs to be taken while processing it. Initially, individual dualband data has been averaged, which helps to identify the central tendency of the data being processed. The averaging may be carried out as

$$y(t) = \frac{1}{T} \int_{t-T}^{t} x(t)\,dt \qquad (5.8)$$

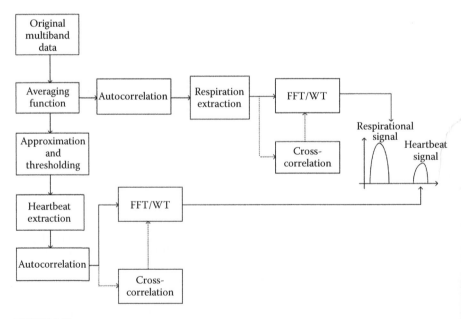

FIGURE 5.14
Algorithm for baseband signal processing.

$x(t)$ is the input signal, $y(t)$ is the averaged signal, and T is the averaging interval. A two-prong strategy is adopted to extract the respiration and heartbeat signals. First, the extraction of the respiration rate signal from the individual dualband data is carried out and the averaged time domain data is autocorrelated to minimize the noise content. Next, a frequency domain transformation is carried out to extract the respiration signal. Smoothing of this signal is achieved with the help of a BPF with passband 0.1 Hz to 0.4 Hz. Finally, the individual dualband data is correlated to achieve a correct identification of the respiration signal. In the next stage, the averaged signal is processed for approximation to extract the heartbeats. Here, a linear approximation function is used for approximation and it is defined as

$$y_L(t) = x(t) - \left[a(t)x(t) + b(t) \right] dt \tag{5.9}$$

where $a(t)$ and $b(t)$ may be estimated using the relations

$$a(t) = \frac{E[XY] - E[X]E[Y]}{E[X^2] - E[X]^2} \tag{5.10}$$

$$b(t) = \frac{E[Y]E[X]^2 - E[XY]E[X]}{E[X^2] - E[X]^2} \tag{5.11}$$

where $E[X]$, $E[Y]$, $E[XY]$, and $E[X]^2$ are the statistical moments calculated over the interval $[(t - T/2) < t < (t + (T/2 + 1))]$. By observing the approximated data, a threshold is selected to decide the heartbeat signals. The individual band data is autocorrelated to minimize the effect of the noise content. The individual band data is then passed through a BPF with a passband from 1 Hz to 3 Hz. A frequency domain transformation is applied to the signals to analyze the individual band data. Further, a cross-correlation is carried out on the dualband data to predict the exact heartbeats. It cancels out the uncorrelated signals from the individual dualband signals and retains only the correlated signals. It provides the accurate prediction of human vital signs.

In the entire analysis, along with the FFT, a wavelet transform (WT) with the Morlet kernel is used to reinforce the detection result. According to Equation 5.7, the bandwidth of the filter for the heartbeat detection is kept from 1 Hz to 3 Hz and that of the respiration is kept from 0.1 Hz to 0.4 Hz. The wide range of the passband is selected to ensure the functionality of the system remain within a tolerable range. Figure 5.15a–f demonstrates the FFT analysis of detected signals with the proposed sensor at a distance of 2 m. Further, WT has been applied on the detected signals for analysis purpose. A similar response has been obtained which validates the proposed concept. Figure 5.16a–c depicts the WT spectrum of the detected signals. The measured results are summarized in Table 5.8.

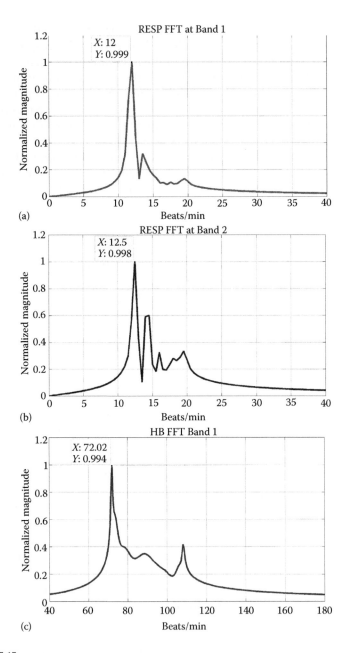

FIGURE 5.15
FFT analysis of the detected signals. (a, b) This provides the FFT of respiration signals at bands 1 and 2, respectively. It shows a clear peak at 12 beats per minute. Figure 5.15c shows that the heartbeats are detected at 72 beats per minute at the lower band.   (*Continued*)

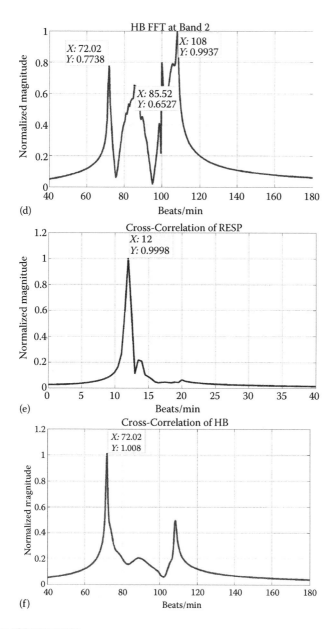

(d)

(e)

(f)

FIGURE 5.15 (CONTINUED)
FFT analysis of the detected signals. However, at the higher band, the detection is not clear and peaks are available at more than one place (Figure 5.15d). This discrepancy is overcome by initiating the cross-correlation between the detected signals at individual bands (Figure 5.15e and f). The respiration peak is clearly obtained at 12 beats per minute, and heartbeats are obtained at 72 beats per minute. The ambiguity in detection is overcome by the cross-correlation of simultaneously detected data. This is the biggest advantage of the detection by using concurrent multiband RF sensor.

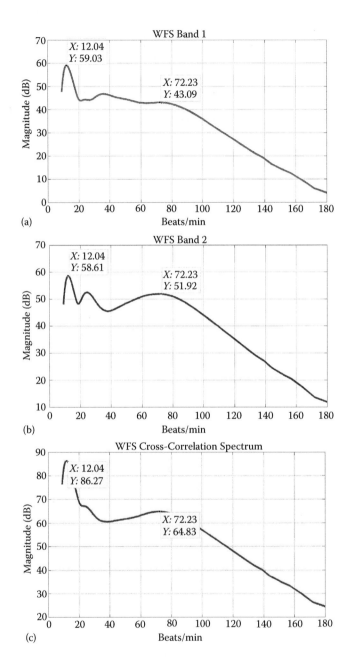

(a)

(b)

(c)

FIGURE 5.16

WT analysis of the detected signals. Further, the detection process is validated with the help of WT of the detected signals at individual bands and their cross-correlation (Figure 5.16a–c). The respiration and heartbeats signals are detected at 12 and 72 beats per minute, respectively. This is similar with the detection with the FFT method. (From Iyer, B., Pathak, N. P., and Ghosh, D., *IEEE Sensor Journal*, 15, 7, 3959–3966, 2015 [98].)

TABLE 5.8

Summary of NIVSD of the RF Sensor

Signal-Processing Technique	Respiration Rate (BPM)	Heartbeats (BPM)
FFT	12	72.04
WT	12.04	72.24

5.6 Conclusions

An RF system based on the Doppler principle for NIVSD has gained popularity in recent years due to its applicability in day-to-day life. A simple and cost-effective answer to meet the trade-off between detection sensitivity and noise content of the baseband signal is provided herein for detection of signals due to heartbeat and respiration in a living human being. Concurrent dualband systems lead to a very compact design with low power consumption. Such a system may be very useful in post-disaster rescue operations, battlefields, and healthcare applications. Due to the non-invasive nature and minimal hardware requirements, the concurrent multiband NIVSD is expected to rapidly acquire importance in day-to-day activities for many people despite their social or financial strata.

6

Occupancy Sensors

6.1 Introduction: Background and Driving Forces

Ascertaining accurate occupancy of a human being inside a room or in a closed space is vital in many day-to-day applications. This chapter describes the application of the proposed concurrent dualband RF sensor as an occupancy sensor. The occupancy is decided by the analysis of baseband signals at individual bands and the correlation between them. The notable advantage of the proposed sensor is the reduction of false alarms due to its concurrent multiband operation.

Occupancy sensors have been used in a variety of daily life applications, from managing air conditioning, home lighting, and heating, to determining the presence of human beings in residential or commercial avenues [101]. Initially limited only to security applications, the occupancy sensors have drawn much attention from researchers and practitioners due to their wide range of applications in the modern era of smart homes and avenues [102]. In the past decades, ultrasonic sensors and passive infrared sensors were the two most commonly used devices for the occupancy sensing [103,104]. However, these sensors were unattractive due to their limitations, such as higher false alarm rate, cost, failure in detection of the stationary subject, and so on.

Respiration and heartbeat are the two predominant characteristics by virtue of which the existence of a human being can be ascertained. With the help of a Doppler-based RF sensor, these vital signs can easily be detected and analyzed non-invasively and continuously over a distance. Hence, this methodology acquired a hot spot in the research arena as compared with its counterparts. With these characteristics, the Doppler radar–based RF sensors emerged as a promising alternative to the existing sensors to minimize false alarms.

Many efforts were initiated toward the development of a low-cost RF occupancy sensor. A 5.8 GHz radar was reported and used as an occupancy sensor. However, the method did not consider heartbeat and respiration rates to confirm the factual presence of human beings. The effort of Lu et al. was limited only to the detection of heartbeat signal and never considered the respiration signal for the analysis [105]. Song et al. and Yavari et al. employed a single-band RF to detect the presence of the human beings [106,107]. Yavari et al. considered the heartbeat as well as the respiration rate for the confirmation of occupancy of a human being.

All the reported methodologies had a limitation of using either the existing RF-based occupancy sensors, which can be characterized based on a single operational band, or specific vital sign detection for deciding the occupancy.

The basic purpose of an occupancy sensor is to confirm the true presence discerning non-human periodic motion, which may result in a false alarm. The confirmation of the occupancy will be more accurate if it has been ascertained by the detection of respiration rate and heartbeat rather than a single vital sign. This will help to reduce false alarms and dead zones in the sensing operation. As the nature of these human vital signs is very weak, the detection must be robust to noise with high sensitivity. Change in the rate of vital signs over a period of time due to irregular body movement and anxiety is a basic tendency of the human beings. Due to this feature, with a single-band RF sensor, there is an enormous possibility that the sensor may generate a false alarms treating it as a human periodic motion. This is the prime disadvantage of the existing single-band RF sensors. This drawback may be overcome by using a multiband operation.

With our proposed concurrent multiband operation, the individual band detection may be carried out simultaneously. Such operation does not suffer from variable measuring conditions. Furthermore, the overall size of the circuit is very compact as a single circuit caters the need of multiband

TABLE 6.1

State-of-the-Art Occupancy Sensor

Contribution	Methodology of Operation	Number of Operational Bands	Concurrent Operation	Subsystem Design	Signal-Processing Technique
Zappi et al. [108]	Infrared	–	No	Commercial ICs were used	–
Caicedo and Pandharipande [105]	Ultrasonic	–	No	Commercial ICs were used	–
Reyes et al. [106]	RF-based	Single-band at 5.8 GHz	No	Own fabricated circuit	–
Song et al. [109]	RF-based	Single-band at 2.4 GHZ	No	Commercial ICs were used	FFT
Yavari et al. [110]	RF-based	Single-band at 2.405 GHz	No	Commercial ICs were used	FFT
Proposed Sensor	RF-based	Dualband at 2.44 and 5.25 GHz	Yes	Own customized concurrent dualband subsystems	FFT/WT

Source: Iyer, B., Pathak, N. P., and Ghosh, D., *IEEE Sensor Journal*, 15, 7, 3959–3966, 2015 [98].

operation. Additionally, it provides a low-cost and less power-hungry option for the occupancy sensing operation [92,96,97]. Hence, a concurrent multi-band RF occupancy sensor is the best alternative to the existing ones. Table 6.1 briefly summarizes the state-of-the-art of occupancy sensor.

6.2 Characterization of the Occupancy Sensor

The working principle of the occupancy sensor is similar to the proposed sensor as described in Section 1.2.1. Figure 6.1 depicts the basic principle of the application of the proposed concurrent multiband RF sensor as an occupancy sensor.

Figure 6.2 shows the setup used in the characterization and performance evaluation of the proposed occupancy sensor. Human subjects may breathe at a constant rate. However, heart rate variability will reveal the truth about one's existence, as it cannot be periodic. Owing to this fact, in the present work, heartbeat along with respiration rate is selected to decide the occupancy.

For experimentation purposes, a 33-year-old male subject was stationed in an indoor environment. The baseband signals were fed to the DAQ module operating at a sampling rate of 37 Hz. The samples were taken for a 10-minute duration. In this analysis, the respiration rate and heartbeat were

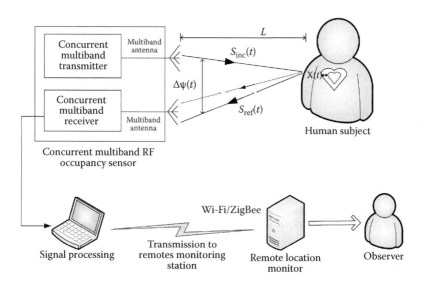

FIGURE 6.1
Working principle of the occupancy sensor. (From Iyer, B., Pathak, N. P., and Ghosh, D., *IEEE Sensor Journal*, 15, 7, 3959–3966, 2015 [98].)

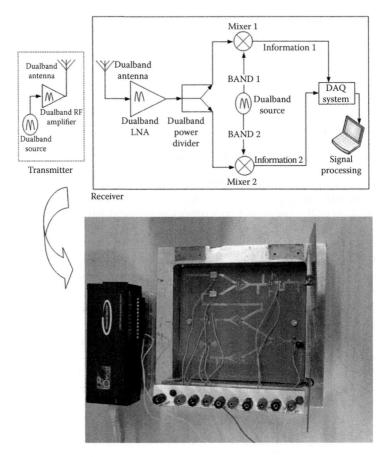

FIGURE 6.2
Characterization and performance evaluation setup for the occupancy sensor.

considered for the confirmation of the occupancy in a particular premise. The occupancy is confirmed only after exact detection of heartbeat and respiration rate. This approach reduces the false alarm rate as with conventional sensors or single-band RF sensors.

Initially, the sensor was operated for the duration of five minutes without any human subject in the vicinity of the sensor. At the end of the fifth minute, a human subject was made to sit in front of the sensor. The data was recorded continuously for the next 5 minutes.

6.2.1 Baseband Signal Processing

Instead of infrared or ultrasonic signals, the operation of the proposed sensor is based on the detection and measurement of the back-scattered EM signals from the human subject. Hence, the usual limitations associated with the conventional sensors are eradicated to confirm the true presence of the human subject. For the first five minutes, the room was kept empty and the signals were captured. At the end of the fifth minute, the human subject was made to enter the room and placed at a distance of 2 m distance from the transceiver antenna. Figure 6.3a and Figure 6.3b depict received signal at the individual band of operation.

The required bandpass filter (BPF) is employed using MATLAB®. This approach helped to overcome the additional hardware and the insertion loss therein. The human respiration rate is generally in the range of 10 to 22 (0.16 Hz to 0.36 Hz) beats per minute with the corresponding heartbeat of 60 to 90 (1 Hz to 1.5 Hz) beats per minute in normal conditions [30].

The passband of the BPF is set accordingly. As it is seen from the received signal at both bands for the first five minutes, there is no evidence of human vital signs since the room is empty. It indicates that the sensor did not capture any non-human motion during the measurements. At the end of the fifth minute, a human being enters the room. The output spectrum clearly shows the ripples around the fifth minute for about 30 seconds till the human being settles down in front of the measurement setup. Signal spectrum obtained in the following time duration shows the human vital signs.

This signal has been further frequency-transferred using FFT to retrieve the human vital sign signals. Figure 6.3c and 6.3d show the FFT spectrum of the detected signal. FFT spectrum of signals received with 2.44 GHz band does not reveal clear understanding of the human vital signs. This kind of response may lead to a false alarm. However, distinct human vital signs are achieved from the signals received at 5.25 GHz. The correlation between the individual band signals (Figure 6.3e) eliminates the ambiguity and provides distinct signals of human respiration and heartbeat. As a result, a more accurate alarm regarding the existence of a human being may be expected. This is the notable advantage of the concurrent multiband RF operation.

Further, the capacity of the proposed sensor has been verified by applying WT over the detected signal. A similar response, as that with FFT method, has been achieved with the use of WT (Figure 6.4).

Table 6.2 summarizes the detection rate of human vital signs using FFT and WT methods. It is found that a fair agreement in detection of the human vital signs is observed by these two methods. The detected signals are further utilized for angle of arrival estimation.

6.2.2 Performance Analysis

The link budget, sensitivity, safety analysis, and detection range estimation of the occupancy sensors are carried out in a similar way as that given in Chapter 5. Additionally, the link budget and sensitivity analysis have been carried out, herein, by placing a wooden board 30 mm in thickness between

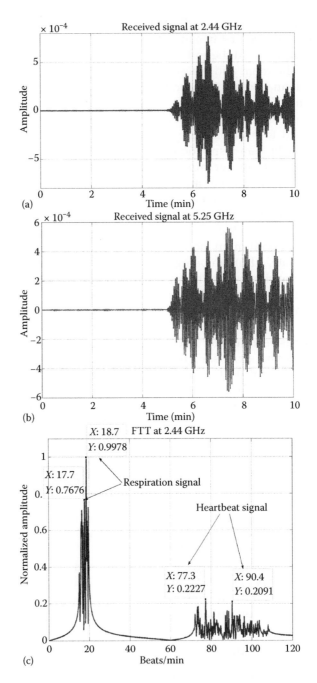

FIGURE 6.3
Received signal at (a) 2.44 GHz and (b) 5.25 GHz band; FFT spectrum of the received signal at (c) 2.44 GHz. (From Iyer, B., Pathak, N. P., and Ghosh, D., *IEEE Sensor Journal*, 15, 7, 3959–3966, 2015 [98].)   (*Continued*)

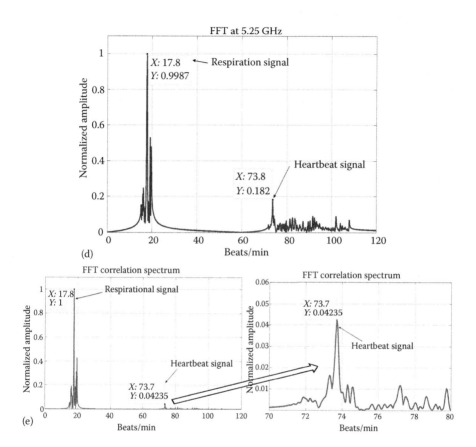

FIGURE 6.3 (CONTINUED)
Received signal at (d) 5.25 GHz, and (e) correlation of the FFT spectrum. (From Iyer, B., Pathak, N. P., and Ghosh, D., *IEEE Sensor Journal*, 15, 7, 3959–3966, 2015 [98].)

the sensor and the human subject. Table 6.3 provides the details of link budget and sensitivity analysis for the proposed sensor.

Since the application is for indoor occupancy detection, it is a must that the number of sensors required for a specific room is estimated. The maximum operational distance and the required number of sensors are estimated as

$$S_N = \frac{RA}{EA} \, units \tag{6.1}$$

where S_N = number of sensor units, RA = room area in m², and EA = exposure area of each sensor (πR_{max}^2). The experiment is initiated in a room of 25 m². Table 6.4 summarizes the sensor requirements in connection with maximum range and transmitted power.

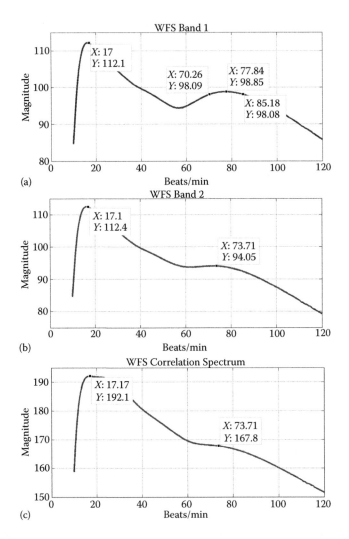

FIGURE 6.4
WT spectrum of the received signal at (a) 2.44 GHz, (b) 5.25 GHz, and (c) correlation of FFT spectrum. (From Iyer, B., Pathak, N. P., and Ghosh, D., *IEEE Sensor Journal*, 15, 7, 3959–3966, 2015 [98].)

TABLE 6.2

VSD Detection by Occupancy Sensor

Methodology	Respiration Rate (BPM)	Heartbeats (BPM)
FFT	17.80	73.7
WT	17.17	73.71

TABLE 6.3

Sensitivity Analysis of the Proposed Sensor

Parameter	Antenna Array (Directive)	Antenna Array (Omnidirective)	Single Patch
Thermal Noise		–174 dBm/Hz	
SNR		20 dB	
Sensitivity		–138.62 dBm	
Received Power (dBm): without obstacle	–64.62	–57.32	–53.92
Received Power (dBm): without obstacle	–81.73	–73.83	–70.23
Link Margin (dBm): without obstacle	74	80.70	84.70
Link Margin (dBm): without obstacle	56.89	64.79	68.39

Source: Iyer, B., Pathak, N. P., and Ghosh, D., *IEEE Sensor Journal*, 15, 7, 3959–3966, 2015 [98].

TABLE 6.4

Output Power and Sensor Unit Requirement

Output Power (dBm)	Maximum Range (meter)	No. of Sensor Unit Requirement
–10	1.3	5
0	2.2	5
5	3	1
10	4	1
20	7.5	1

Source: Iyer, B., Pathak, N. P., and Ghosh, D., *IEEE Sensor Journal*, 15, 7, 3959–3966, 2015 [98].

6.2.3 Indoor Location Detection of Human Subject

The location or position of the human subject inside a room can be ascertained by calculating the angle of arrival. Many efforts were reported in the literature to estimate the angle of arrival. However, few have concentrated on the human VSD-centric approach while estimating the direction of arrival (DOA). Table 6.5 provides the state-of-the-art of the human VSD-centric angle of arrival detection. The DOA is estimated by using multiple signal classification (MUSIC) algorithm [109].

It is quite possible that in practical situations, such as in hospitals or when victims are buried under debris/rubble, this might not exactly face up to the sensor antenna. Measurement and estimation of the heartbeat and respiration rate using a Doppler-based RF sensor are possible, even if the human chest is not pointed directly toward the sensor [54]. In comparison to a single-band sensor as reported by Li et al. in [54], we have employed a concurrent dualband sensor for detection purposes. Due to the advantages of concurrent multiband operation, the possibility of a false signal generation has been mitigated in the present approach. The human being may be in

TABLE 6.5

Comparison of DoA Systems

Parameter	Isar et al. [110]	Yong et al. [111]	Proposed Sensor
No. of operational bands	One: 2.4 GHz	One: 2.4 GHz	Two: Concurrent 2.44 and 5.25 GHz
Switching mechanism	RF switch–based operation	PLL-based switch operation	Not required
No. of system employed	One: A separate transmitter and receiver	One: A separate transmitter and receiver	One: A concurrent dualband transceiver
MIMO operation support	No	Yes	Yes
Subsystem used	Commercial subsystems	Commercial subsystems	Indigenously customized concurrent dualband subsystems

Source: Iyer, B., Pathak, N. P., and Ghosh, D., *IEEE Sensor Journal*, 15, 7, 3959–3966, 2015 [98].

any orientation, as shown in Figure 6.5. For the present analysis, the human subject under test was distanced 2 meters and positioned at different angles away from the transceiver. The sampling rate and sampling interval are kept the same as that of occupancy measurement. The received data will be in the form of

$$y[n] = [y_1 + \ldots\ldots + y_k] \tag{6.2}$$

Here, y_k is the baseband signal recorded at Band 1 and Band 2, and n is the total number of samples acquired. With the acquired multiband data, a DoA

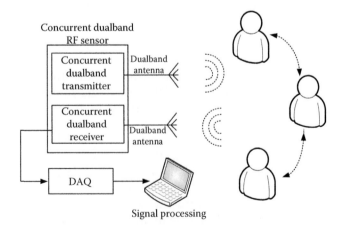

FIGURE 6.5

Conceptual setup of measurement of DoA. (From Iyer, B., Pathak, N. P., and Ghosh, D., *IEEE Sensor Journal*, 15, 7, 3959–3966, 2015 [98].)

spectrum is calculated. The peaks in the pseudospectrum are the DoAs (angle of arrival, AoA) for the human subject under test. For the present analysis, the human subject under test was distanced 2 m and positioned manually at 30°, 90°, 130°, and 160° away from the transmitting antenna such that the human chest was not directly pointed toward the transmitting antenna. The placement of the human subject at these angles was done manually, and this method had its own limitations. Figure 6.6 shows the estimated DoA at different angles with the proposed sensor. It shows that the human subject is positioned at an angle of 31.5°, 91°, 127°, and 166° from the sensor.

The difference in the actual and measured angles may be attributed to the manual measurement of angles for the placement of the human subject. Here, only one peak has been observed since only a single receiver antenna was employed. The catch line advantage of the present detection work lies in the multiband operation of the sensor system. Data in the individual frequency band was assumed to be received from individual antennas, which are correlated to arrive at a final conclusion. This approach is found to be very useful in the tracking of multiple objects or continuously moving objects. Thus, the correlation of the multiband data not only provides the correct estimation of DoA, but it also reduces the motion artifacts, clutters, and allied noise. The efforts of Yong et al. [111] achieved MIMO operation by two different systems, while in our proposed approach, MIMO operation was achieved in

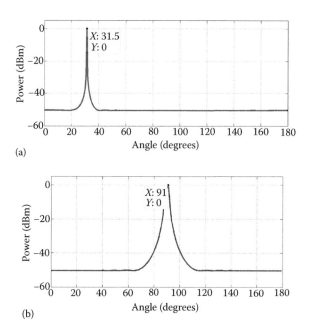

(a)

(b)

FIGURE 6.6
DOA detection at (a) 30° and (b) 90°. (From Iyer, B., Pathak, N. P., and Ghosh, D., *IEEE Sensor Journal*, 15, 7, 3959–3966, 2015 [98].) (*Continued*)

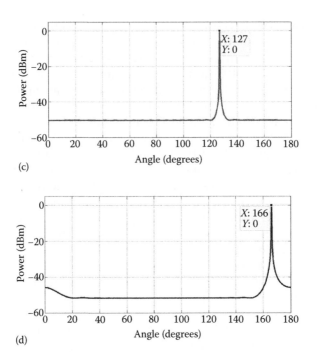

(c)

(d)

FIGURE 6.6 (CONTINUED)
DOA detection at (c) 130° and (d) 160°. (From Iyer, B., Pathak, N. P., and Ghosh, D., *IEEE Sensor Journal*, 15, 7, 3959–3966, 2015 [98].)

a single sensor unit simultaneously operating in multiple frequency bands. The DoA estimation is very useful for law enforcement agencies to identify the number of persons in a closed space or for through-wall detection.

6.3 Conclusions

A dual-input and dual-output concurrent dualband RF sensor has been used to sense the presence of a human being inside a room. The inability of the existing occupancy sensors to detect a stationary subject is alleviated in this RF sensor. The false alarms and the dead spots in the sensing operation are effectively reduced by using both heartbeat and respiration rate signals to sense human presence. Due to concurrent dualband operations, the proposed sensor has a very compact size and low power consumptions. This sensor will be very useful in home care for elderly people and for law enforcement agencies to decide the human occupancy of a room.

7

Conclusions and Future Scope

7.1 Conclusions

In this book, a concurrent dualband non-invasive vital sign–monitoring sensor system is proposed and demonstrated. The proposed system is devised on the popular Doppler shift theory and simultaneous operation over two frequency bands, namely, the 2.44 GHz and 5.25 GHz bands.

Here, the baseband signal after the mixer stage is generally proportional to chest disarticulation and thus contains information about movement due to heartbeat and respiration. Using this information, the existence of a human life can be ascertained. Based on this notion, a non-invasive heart and respiration monitor is developed.

There are various technical obstructions in designing an NIVSD system, such as the influence of clutter noise and phase noise, the harmonics, DC offset, and null point problems. Various academicians and researchers had suggested many techniques to overcome these challenges whereby a stable and reliable detection has been achieved.

For people who have a large chest wall movement due to breathing, a lower frequency system is better. For increased detection sensitivity, higher-band systems are preferred. However, in human vital sign detection applications, the existing single-band systems cannot provide the aforementioned attributes simultaneously. The challenge to bridge the trade-off between lower noise content and higher detection accuracy was unattended before the initiation of this research work. This challenge has motivated the design and development of a concurrent multiband RF sensor.

The entire work is divided into four parts. In the first part of the system design and development, a concurrent dualband antenna of both omnidirectional and directional types was designed to operate simultaneously at the designated bands. Apart from this, concurrent dualband LNA and WPD were also designed as the subsystems for the proposed system.

In the second stage, simulation verification of the proposed system with an ADS platform was carried out. Here, measured S2P files of the subsystems were used for simulation. Then a measurement prototype was established with the VNA and two concurrent dualband patch antennas. The setup had shown an accurate detection up to a distance of 1 m. With this experience, a measurement setup was developed with the help of our own customized concurrent dualband subsystems and off-the-shelf laboratory equipment. The individual subsystems were connected together via cables and connectors. The setup showed an accuracy of detection up to 2 m. However, it suffered from a lot of noise in the received data.

Based on the experience of the previous two stages, the problem of noise content was overcome by fabricating the entire circuitry on a single substrate. This approach minimized the noise in comparison to the previous versions as the need of cables and connectors are eliminated. Further, a novel method to process the noisy baseband signal was developed. With the help of the fabricated system and signal processing, it was observed that the noise content is significantly reduced and distinct peaks of respiration and heartbeat were observed at both the designated bands as well as after correlation of the individual band data.

Efforts are being initiated toward the design and development of a portable, handheld complete sensor system. Such systems can be very useful in postdisaster rescue operations, battlefields, and in healthcare applications. Due to its non-invasive nature and minimal hardware requirements, a concurrent multiband NIVSD is expected to rapidly acquire importance in day-to-day activities for many people, despite their social or financial strata.

7.2 Future Scope

7.2.1 Reconfigurable/Tunable Concurrent Dualband NIVSD

A reconfigurable/tunable NIVSD is to be designed to operate between the entire individual WLAN bands (that is, 2.14 GHz to 2.45 GHz and 5.15 GHz to 5.35 GHz). This will help the user choose an optimal frequency ratio for a particular operation. Figure 7.1 shows the conceptual diagram and measurement prototype for the reconfigurable concurrent dualband RF system for non-invasive human vital sign detection. The selection of the proper frequency ratio plays a key role for the accuracy and sensitivity of a concurrent multiband RF system employed for NIVSD application. The performance of such concurrent multiband RF systems can be further improved by incorporation of the concept of reconfigurability. It provides the flexibility to select the individual operational bands, depending on the need of the application(s). This novelty may be achieved by designing individual reconfigurable subsystems. The additional feature of reconfigurability provides the benefit of selecting the best frequency ratio for a particular operation by tuning the frequency of operation at both bands concurrently.

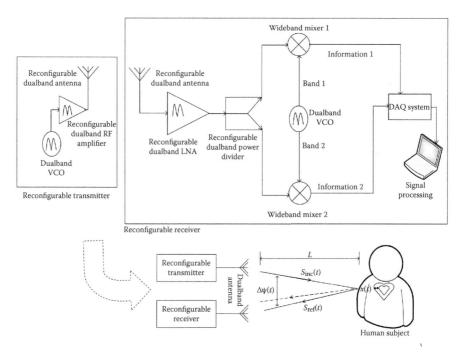

FIGURE 7.1
Conceptual diagram of a reconfigurable multiband RF sensor for human VSD. (From Iyer, B., Pathak, N., Ghosh, D., 2014 IEEE Region 10 Humanitarian Technology Conference (R10 HTC), Chennai, India, pp. 112–119, 2014 [21].)

The proper selection of the frequency ratio provides a twofold advantage over the static multiband RF radios. First, the noise performance and sensitivity can be improved; second, improved accuracy can be obtained in the detection of weak human vital sign signals. All these features can be obtained via multiband RF systems with the incorporation of a varactor diode as a tuning element. By controlling the bias voltage of the varactor diode, desired tuning can be achieved.

7.2.2 Handheld Concurrent Dualband Human Life Tracking Sensor

In real-time applications, it is not always feasible to carry bulky tracking systems for sensing human life. Hence, there is a need to develop a portable handheld device to sense human vital signs. This may be possible by indigenously comprehended concurrent dualband subsystems to replace off-the-shelf laboratory equipment. A partial effort was initiated by fabricating a transceiver prototype on a single substrate. Figure 5.12 depicts the prototype of the proposed portable handheld concurrent dualband sensor for human vital sign detection. In the future, this prototype is to be converted into a fully functioning handheld device for NIVSD applications.

References

1. J. C. Lin. 1975. Noninvasive microwave measurement of respiration. *Proceedings of IEEE*, 63, 10, p. 1530.
2. D. Droitcour, O. Lubecke, V. Lubecke, J. Lin, and G. Kovac. 2004. Range correlation and I/Q performance benefits in single-chip silicon Doppler radars for noncontact cardiopulmonary monitoring. *IEEE Transactions on Microwave Theory and Techniques*, 52, 3, pp. 838–848.
3. C. Stezer, G. Diskus, K. Lubke, and H. Thim. 1999. Microwave position sensor with sub millimeter accuracy. *IEEE Transactions on Microwave Theory and Technique*, 47, 12, pp. 2621–2624.
4. M. Shaji and M. Akhtar. 2013. Microwave coplanar sensor system for detecting contamination in food products. In *Proceedings of IEEE MTT–S International Microwave and RF Conference* (IMaRC–2013), New Delhi, India, pp. 1–4.
5. A. Jha and M. Akhtar. 2013. Automated RF measurement system for detecting adulteration in edible fluids. In *Proceedings of IEEE Applied Electromagnetics Conference* (AEMC-13), Bhubaneswar, India, pp. 18–20.
6. O. Lubecke, J. Lin, B. Park, C. Li, W. Massagram, V. Lubecke, A. Madsen. 2008. Battlefield triage life signs detection techniques. In *Proceedings of SPIE Defense and Security Symposium*, Radar Sensor Technology XII, 6947, 69470J.
7. A. Aubert, B. Seps, and F. Beckers. 2003. Heart rate variability in athletes. *Sports Medicine*, 33, 12, pp. 89–919.
8. P. Kumar and T. Kumar. 2012. A novel approach for clutter reduction in through-the-wall UWB radar imaging. *IETE Journal of Research*, 58, 5, pp. 341–346.
9. Y. An, B. Jang, and J. Yook. 2010. Detection of human vital signs and estimation of direction of arrival using multiple doppler radars. *Journal of the Korean Institute of Electromagnetic*, 10, 4, pp. 250–255.
10. C. Gu and J. Lin. 2010. Instrument-based noncontact Doppler radar vital sign detection system using heterodyne digital quadrature demodulation architecture. *IEEE Transaction on Instrumentation and Measurement*, 59, 6, pp. 1580–1588.
11. Y. Xiao, J. Lin, O. Lubecke, and V. Lubecke. 2006. Frequency tuning technique for remote detection of heartbeat and respiration using low-power double-sideband transmission in the Ka-Band. *IEEE Transactions on Microwave Theory and Techniques*, 54, 5, pp. 2023–2032.
12. X. Yu, C. Li, and J. Lin. 2011. Two-dimensional noncontact vital sign detection using doppler radar array approach. *IEEE MTT-S International Microwave Symposium Digest* (MTT-11), Baltimore, MD, pp. 1–4.
13. S. Guan, J. Rice, C. Li, and G. Wang. 2014. Bridge deflection monitoring using small, low-cost radar sensors. *Structures Congress*, Boston, MA, pp. 2853–2862.
14. Rehabilitation of Villages Devastated in Uttarakhand Flood. U Turn Foundation. Available at http://uturnfoundation.org/wputurn/rehabilitation-of-villages-devastated-in-uttarakhand-flood.
15. CodeBlueProject. Available at http://www. eecs.harvard.edu/~mdw/proj/code blue.

16. Prince Rescued. KBK Infographics. Available at http://im.rediff.com/news/2006/jul/23prince.gif.
17. RANGE-R® Theory of Operation. RANGE-R®. Available at http://www.ranger.com/tech/theory.htm.
18. Target Heart Rates. American Heart Association (AHA). Available at www.heart.org/HEARTORG/GettingHealthy.
19. R. Page. 1962. The early history of radar. *Proceedings of IRE*, 50, 5, pp. 1232–1236.
20. M. Guarnieri. 2010. The early history of radar. *IEEE Industrial Electronics Magazine*, 4, 3, pp. 36–42.
21. B. Iyer, N. Pathak, and D. Ghosh. 2014. Reconfigurable multiband concurrent RF system for non-invasive human vital sign detection. *2014 IEEE Region 10 Humanitarian Technology Conference* (R10 HTC), Chennai, India, pp. 112–119.
22. A. Tariq and H. Shiraz. 2010. Doppler Radar vital signs monitoring using wavelet transform. *Proceedings of Antennas and Propagation Conference*, Loughborough, UK, pp. 293–296.
23. A. Madsen, N. Petrochilos, O. Lubecke, and V. Lubecke. 2008. Signal processing methods for Doppler radar heart rate monitoring. *Signal Processing Techniques for Knowledge Extraction and Information Fusion*, pp. 121–140.
24. E. Sharifahmadian and A. Ahmadian. 2009. Adaptive signal processing algorithm for remote detection of heart rate (HR) using ultra-wideband waveforms based on principal component analysis. *Annual International Conference of the IEEE Engineering in Medicine and Biology Society* (EMBC 2009), Minnesota, pp. 5717–5720.
25. M. Rahman, B. Jang, and K. Kim. 2008. A new digital signal processor for Doppler radar cardiopulmonary monitoring system. *International Conference on Electrical and Computer Engineering*, Dhaka, pp. 76–79.
26. M. Vergara, N. Petrochilos, O. Lubecke, A. Madsen, and V. Lubecke. 2008. Blind source separation of human body motion using direct conversion Doppler radar. *IEEE MTT–S International Microwave Symposium Digest*, Atlanta, pp. 1321–1324.
27. M. Vergara, O. Lubecke and V. Lubecke. 2008. DC information preservation for cardiopulmonary monitor utilizing CW Doppler radar. *IEEE Engineering in Medicine and Biology Society Annual International Conference*, Vancouver, pp. 1246–1249.
28. T. Chin, K. Lin, S. Chang, and C. Chang. 2010. A fast clutter cancellation method in quadrature Doppler radar for noncontact vital signal detection. *IEEE MTT–S International Microwave Symposium Digest*, Anaheim, California, pp. 764–767.
29. J. Cheng, J. Yeh, H. Yang, J. Tsai, J. Lin, and T. Huang. 2012. 40-GHz vital sign detection of heartbeat using synchronized motion technique for respiration signal suppression. *Proceedings of the 42nd European Microwave Conference*, Amsterdam, The Netherlands, pp. 21–24.
30. K. Kurokawa. 1973. Injection locking of microwave solid state oscillators. *Proceedings of IEEE*, 61, pp. 1386–1410.
31. B. Razavi. 1999. RF transmitter architectures and circuits. *IEEE Custom Integrated Circuits Conference*, pp. 197–204.
32. T. Yamawaki et al. 1997. A 2.7-V GSM RF Transceiver IC. IEEE *Journal of Solid state Circuits*, 32, pp. 2089–2096.
33. A. Edwin. 1921. A new system of short wave amplification. *Proceedings of the IRE*, Institute of Radio Engineers, New York, 9, 1, pp. 3–11. Retrieved October 22, 2013.

34. A. Singh and V. Lubecke. 2009. Respiratory monitoring using a Doppler radar with passive harmonic tags to reduce interference from environmental clutter. *IEEE Engineering in Medicine and Biology Society Annual International Conference,* Minneapolis, Minnesota, pp. 3837–3840.

35. C. Wu and Z. Huang. 2008. Using the phase change of a reflected microwave to detect a human subject behind a barrier. *IEEE Transactions on Biomedical Engineering,* 55, 1, pp. 267–272.

36. C. Gu, J. Long, J. Huangfu, S. Qiao, W. Cui, W. Ma, and L. Ran. 2008. An instrument-built Doppler radar for sensing vital signs. *8th International Symposium on Antennas, Propagation and EM Theory,* Kunming, pp. 1398–1401.

37. F. Wang, C. Li, C. Hsiao, T. Horng, J. Lin, K. Peng, J. Jau, J. Li, and C. Chen. 2010. An injection-locked detector for concurrent spectrum and vital sign sensing. IEEE MTT–S International Microwave Symposium Digest, Anaheim, California, pp. 768–771.

38. I. Immoreev and T. Tao. 2008. UWB Radar for patient monitoring. *IEEE Aerospace and Electronic Systems Magazine,* 23, 11, pp. 11–18.

39. L. Anitori, A. Jong, and F. Nennie. 2009. FMCW radar for life-sign detection. *IEEE Radar Conference,* Pasadena, California, pp. 1–6.

40. A. Wiesner. 2009. A multifrequency interferometric CW radar for vital signs detection. IEEE Radar Conference, Pasadena, California, pp. 1–4.

41. A. Droitcour, V. Lubecke, J. Lin, and O. Lubecke. 2001. A microwave radio for Doppler radar sensing of vital signs. IEEE MTT–S International Microwave Symposium Digest, Phoenix, Arizona, pp. 175–178.

42. A. Droitcour, O. Lubecke, V. Lubecke, and J. Lin. 2002. 0.25 μm CMOS and BiCMOS single chip direct conversion Doppler radars for remote sensing of vital signs. *IEEE International Solid–State Circuits Conference Digest* (ISSCC–2002), San Francisco, pp. 348–349.

43. K. Chen, Y. Huang, J. Zhang, and A. Norman. 2000. Microwave life-detection systems for searching human subjects under earthquake rubble and behind barrier. *IEEE Transactions on Biomedical Engineering,* 47, 1, pp. 105–114.

44. S. Dragan, B. Park, and O. Lubecke. 2007. Experimental evaluation of multiple antenna techniques for remote sensing of physiological motion. *IEEE MTT–S International Microwave Symposium,* Honolulu, pp. 1735–1738.

45. X. Yu and J. Lin. 2010. Noise analysis for noncontact vital sign detectors. 11th IEEE Annual Wireless and Microwave Technology Conference (WAMICON), Melbourne, Florida, pp. 1–4.

46. H. Kuo, H. Wang, P. Wang, and H. Chuang. 2011. 60-GHz millimeter-wave life detection system with clutter canceller for remote human vital-signal sensing. IEEE MTT–S International Microwave Workshop Series on Millimeter Wave Integration Technologies (IMWS), Sitges, pp. 93–96.

47. A. Lazaro, D. Girbau, and R. Villarino. 2014. Techniques for clutter suppression in the presence of body movements during the detection of respiratory activity through UWB radars. *Sensors,* 14, pp. 2595–2618.

48. Y. Xiao, J. Lin, O. Lubecke, and V. Lubecke. 2005. A Ka-band low power Doppler radar system for remote detection of cardiopulmonary motion. In *Proceedings of the 27th IEEE Annual Conference on Engineering in Medicine and Biology,* Shanghai, China, pp. 7151–7154.

49. B. Park, O. Lubecke, and V. Lubecke. 2007. Arctangent demodulation with DC offset compensation in quadrature Doppler radar receiver systems. *IEEE Transactions on Microwave Theory and Techniques*, 55, 5, pp. 1073–1079.
50. C. Li, Y. Xiao, and J. Lin. 2007. Design guidelines for radio frequency non-contact vital sign detection. *Proceedings of the 29th Annual International Conference of the IEEE EMBS*, Lyon–France, pp. 1651–1654.
51. X. Yu, C. Li, and J. Lin. 2011. Two-dimensional noncontact vital sign detection using Doppler radar array approach. *IEEE MTT–S International Microwave Symposium Digest*, Baltimore, pp. 1–4.
52. C. Gu, C. Li, J. Lin, J. Long, J. Huangfu, and L. Ran. 2010. Instrument-based noncontact Doppler radar vital sign detection system using heterodyne digital quadrature demodulation architecture. *IEEE Transactions on Instrumentation and Measurement*, 59, 6, pp. 1580–1588.
53. Y. Immoreev and S. Samkov. 2002. Ultra-wideband radar for remote measuring of main parameters of patient's vital activity. *IEEE International Workshop on the Ultra Wideband and Ultra Short Impulse Signals* (UWBUSIS–02), Kharkov, Ukraine, pp. 1–4.
54. C. Li, Y. Xiao, and J. Lin. 2006. Experiment and spectral analysis of a low-power Ka-Band heartbeat detector measuring from four sides of a human body. *IEEE Transactions on Microwave Theory and Techniques*, 54, 12, pp. 4464–4471.
55. C. Li and J. Lin. 2008. Random body movement cancellation in Doppler radar vital sign detection. *IEEE Transactions on Microwave Theory and Techniques*, 56, 12, pp. 3143–3152.
56. D. Girbau, A. Lazaro, A. Ramos, and R. Villarino. 2012. Remote sensing of vital signs using a Doppler radar and diversity to overcome null detection. *IEEE Sensors Journal*, 12, 3, pp. 512–518.
57. J. Long, C. Gu, Y. Tao, J. Huangfu, S. Qiao, W. Cui, W. Ma, and L. Ran. 2008. A novel direct-conversion structure for non-contact vital sign detection system. 8th International Symposium on Antennas, Propagation and EM Theory (ISAPE–2008), Kunming, pp. 1282–1285.
58. L. Chioukh, H. Boutayeb, D. Deslandes, and K. Wu. 2010. Multi-frequency radar systems for monitoring vital signs. *Proceedings of Asia–Pacific Microwave Conference* (APMC), Yokohama, pp. 1669–1672.
59. R. Fletcher and J. Han. 2009. Low-cost differential front-end for Doppler radar vital sign monitoring. *IEEE MTT–S International Microwave Symposium Digest*, Boston, Massachusetts, pp. 1325–1328.
60. J. Oum, D. Kim, and S.Hong. 2008. Two frequency radar sensor for non-contact vital signal monitor. *IEEE MTT–S International Microwave Symposium Digest*, Atlanta, Georgia, pp. 919–922.
61. G. Deschamps. 1953. Microstrip microwave antennas. *3rd UASF Symposium on Antennas*.
62. R. Garg and K. Ray. 2003. *Microstrip Line Antenna Design*. Artech House, USA.
63. A. Rathore, R. Nilavalan, H. Tarboush, and T. Peter. 2010. Compact dual-band (2.4/5.2 GHz) monopole antenna for WLAN applications. International Workshop on Antenna Technology, pp. 1–4.
64. Z. Park, C. Li, and J. Lin. 2009. A broadband microstrip antenna with improved gain for noncontact vital sign radar detection. *IEEE Antennas and Wireless Propagation Letters*, 8, pp. 939–942.

65. Z. Park and J. Lin. 2016. A beam steering broadband microstrip antenna for noncontact vital sign radar detection. *IEEE Antennas and Wireless Propagation Letters*, 10, pp. 235–238.
66. W. Swelam, M. Soliman, A. Gomaa, and T. Taha. 2010. Compact dual-band microstrip patch array antenna for MIMO 4G communication systems. *IEEE Antennas and Propagation Society International Symposium* (APSURSI–2010), Toronto, pp. 1–4.
67. Y. Khraisat. 2012. Design of 4 elements rectangular microstrip patch antenna with high gain for 2.4 *GHz* applications. *Modern Applied Science*, 6, 1, pp. 68–74.
68. C. Ghosh and S. Parui. 2010. Design, analysis and optimization of a slotted microstrip patch antenna array at frequency 5.25 GHz for WLAN–SDMA system. *International Journal on Electrical Engineering and Informatics*, 2, 2, pp. 102–112.
69. J. Chitra and V. Nagarajan. 2013. Double L-slot microstrip patch antenna array for WiMax and WLAN applications. *Computer and Electrical Engineering*, 39, 3, pp. 1026–1041.
70. K. Lau, K. Lukand, and K. Lee. 2001. Wideband U-slot microstrip patch antenna array. *IEEE Proceedings on Microwaves, Antennas and Propagation*, 148, 1, pp. 41–44.
71. R. Li, T. Wu, and M. Tentzeris. 2008. A dual-band unidirectional coplanar antenna for 2.4–5 GHz wireless applications. *Asia–Pacific Microwave Conference* (APMC–08), Macau, pp. 1–4.
72. B. Iyer, N. Pathak, and D. Ghosh. 2014. Concurrent dualband patch antenna array for non-invasive human vital sign detection application. *IEEE Asia-Pacific Conference on Applied Electromagnetics*, Malaysia, pp. 150–153.
73. J. Baena et al. 2005. Equivalent-circuit models for split-ring resonators and complementary split-ring resonators coupled to planar transmission lines. *IEEE Transactions on Microwave Theory and Techniques*, 53, 4, pp. 1451–1461.
74. R. Munson. 1974. Conformal microstrip antennas and microstrip phased arrays. *IEEE Transactions on Antennas and Propagation*, AP–22, 1, pp. 74–78.
75. B. Iyer, A. Kumar, and N. P. Pathak. Design and analysis of concurrent dual-band subsystems for WLAN applications. *International Conference on Signal Processing and Communication* (ICSC–2013), Noida, India, pp. 57–61.
76. E. Wilkinson. An n-way hybrid power divider. 1960. *IRE Transactions on Microwave Theory and Techniques*, 8, 1, pp. 116–118.
77. C. Monzon. 2003. A small dual-frequency transformer in two sections. *IEEE Transactions on Microwave Theory Techniques*, 51, 4, pp. 1157–1161.
78. S. Srisathit, M. Chongcheawchamnan, and A. Worapishet. 2003. Design and realization of dual-band 3 dB power divider based on two-section transmission-line topology. *Electronics Letters*, 39, 9, pp. 723–724.
79. L. Wu, H. Yilmaz, T. Bitzer, A. Pascht, and M. Berroth. 2005. A dual-frequency Wilkinson power divider: For a frequency and its first harmonic. *IEEE Microwave and Wireless Component Letters*, 5, 2, pp. 107–109.
80. Z. Jia, Q. Zhu, and F. Ao. 2006. A 2-way broad-band microstrip matched power divider. *Proceedings of International Conference on Communications, Circuits and Systems*, Guilin, 4, pp. 2592–2596.
81. S. Oh et al. 2007. An unequal Wilkinson power divider with variable dividing ratio. *IEEE MTT–S International Microwave Symposium*, Honolulu, Hawaii, pp. 411–414.

82. M. Cheng and F. Wong. 2007. A NewWilkinson power divider design for dualband application. *IEEE Microwave and Wireless Components Letters*, 17, 9, pp. 664–666.

83. A. Naghavi, M. Aghmiyouni, M. Jahanbakht, and A. Neyestanak. 2010. Hybrid wideband microstrip Wilkinson power divider based on lowpass filter optimized using particle swarm method. *Journal of Electromagnetic Waves and Applications*, 24, 14–15, pp. 1877–1886.

84. B. Iyer. 2017. Characterisation of Concurrent Multiband RF Transceiver for WLAN Applications. *Advances in Intelligent Systems Research*, 137, pp. 834–846.

85. V. Dao, B. Choi, and C. Park. 2006. Dual-band LNA for 2.4/5.2 GHz applications. Asia–Pacific Microwave Conference (APMC), Yokohama, pp. 413–416.

86. S. Yoo and H. Yoo. 2007. A compact dualband LNA using self-matched capacitor. IEEE International Workshop on Radio–Frequency Integration Technology (RFIT), Rasa, Sentosa, pp. 227–230.

87. M. Martins, J. Fernandes, and M. Silva. 2007. Techniques for dual-band LNA design using cascode switching and inductor magnetic coupling. *IEEE International Symposium on Circuits and Systems* (ISCAS–2007), New Orleans, Louisiana, pp. 1449–1452.

88. H. Hashemi and A. Hajimiri. 2002. Concurrent multiband low-noise amplifiers: Theory, design, and applications. *IEEE Transactions on Microwave Theory and Techniques*, 50, 1, pp. 288–301.

89. B. Iyer and N. P. Pathak. 2014. Concurrent dual-band LNA for non-invasive vital sign detection. *Microwave and Optical Technology Letters*, 56, 2, pp. 391–394.

90. D. Pozar. 2007. *Microwave Engineering*, 3rd ed. Wiley, India.

91. M. Amor, A. Fakhfakh, H. Mnif, and M. Loulou. 2006. Dual band CMOS LNA design with current reuse topology. *International Conference on Design and Test of Integrated Systems in Nanoscale Technology* (DTIS 2006), Tunis, pp. 57–61.

92. B. Iyer, A. Kumar, N. P. Pathak, and D. Ghosh. 2013. Concurrent multiband RF system for search and rescue of human life during natural calamities. *International Microwave and Radio frequency Conference* (IMaRC–2013). New Delhi, India, pp. 1–4.

93. H. Atwater. 1983. Microstrip reactive circuit elements. *IEEE Transactions on Microwave Theory and Techniques*, 31, 6, pp. 488–491.

94. Y. Cassivi and K. Wu. 2003. Low-cost microwave oscillator using substrate integrated waveguide cavity. *IEEE Microwave and Wireless Components Letters*, 13, 2, pp. 48–50.

95. C. Chou and J. Andrea, subcommittee co-chairs. 2006. IEEE standard for safety levels with respect to human exposure to radio frequency electromagnetic field, 3 kHz to 300 GHz. IEEE Std. C95.1TM–2005. Revision of IEEE Std C95.1–1991. IEEE, New York.

96. B. Iyer, M. Garg, N. P. Pathak, and D. Ghosh. 2013. Concurrent dualband RF system for human respiration rate and heartbeat detection. *Proceedings of International Conference of Information and Communication Technologies* (ICT–2013). Tamilnadu, India, pp. 563–567.

97. B. Iyer, M. Garg, N. P. Pathak, and D. Ghosh. 2013. Contactless detection and analysis of human vital signs using concurrent dual-band RF system. *Elsevier Procedia Engineering*, 64, pp. 185–194.

98. B. Iyer, N. P. Pathak, and D. Ghosh. 2015. Dual input dual output RF sensor for indoor human occupancy and position monitoring. *IEEE Sensor Journal*, 15, 7, pp. 3959–3966.

99. R. Robergs and R. Landwehr. 2002. The surprising history of the *HRmax=220*-age equation. *Journal of Exercise Physiology*, 5, 2, pp. 1–10.

100. J. Adams. 1988. How to design an invisible aircraft. *IEEE Spectrum*, pp. 26–31.

101. G. Vishal and N. Bansal. 2000. Smart occupancy sensors to reduce energy consumption. *Energy Buildings*, 32, 1, pp. 81–87.

102. Aricent Inc. 2010. Market report. Home energy management—beyond the numbers. Available at www.aricent.com/pdf/Aricent_Group_HEMS.pdf.

103. P. Zappi, E. Farella, and L. Benini. 2007. Enhancing the spatial resolution of presence detection in a PIR based wireless surveillance network. *IEEE Conference on Advanced Video and Signal Based Surveillance* (AVSS–2007), London, UK, pp. 295–300.

104. D. Caicedo and A. Pandharipande. 2012. Ultrasonic array sensor for indoor presence detection. *20th European Signal Processing Conference* (EUSIPCO 2012), Bucharest, Romania, pp. 175–179.

105. L. Lu, C. Li, and D. Lie. 2010. Experimental demonstration of noncontact pulse wave velocity monitoring using multiple Doppler radar sensors. *Annual International Conference of Engineering in Medicine and Biology Society* (EMBC–2010), Buenos Aires, Argentina, pp. 5010–5013.

106. C. Song, E. Yavari, A. Singh, O. Lubecke, and V. Lubecke. 2012. Detection sensitivity and power consumption vs. operation modes using system-on-chip based Doppler radar occupancy sensor. *IEEE Topical Conference on Biomedical Wireless Technologies, Networks, and Sensing Systems* (BioWireleSS–12), Santa Clara, California, pp. 17–20.

107. E. Yavari, H. Jou, V. Lubecke, and O. Lubecke. 2013. Doppler radar sensor for occupancy monitoring. *IEEE Radio and Wireless Symposium* (RWS), Austin, pp. 316–318.

108. G. Reyes, D. Wang, R. Nair, C. Li, X. Li, and J. Lin. 2012. VitalTrack: A Doppler radar sensor platform for monitoring activity levels. *IEEE Topical Conference on Biomedical Wireless Technologies, Networks, and Sensing Systems* (BioWireleSS–2012), Santa Clara, California, pp. 29–32.

109. S. Chandran. 2006. Advances in direction-of-arrival estimation. Artech House, Inc., Norwood, Massachusetts.

110. M. Isar, E. Yavari, and O. Lubecke. 2013. A low-cost simple RF front end using time–domain multiplexing for direction of arrival estimation of physiological signals. *IEEE MTT–S International Microwave Symposium Digest* (IMS–2013), Seattle, Washington, pp. 1–4.

111. A. Yong, B. Jang, and J. Yook. 2010. Detection of human vital signs and estimation of direction of arrival using multiple Doppler radars. *Journal of Korean Institute of Electromagnetic Engineering and Science*, 10, 4, pp. 250–254.

Index

Page numbers followed by f and t indicate figures and tables, respectively.

For Product Safety Concerns and Information please contact our EU
representative GPSR@taylorandfrancis.com Taylor & Francis Verlag GmbH,
Kaufingerstraße 24, 80331 München, Germany

Printed and bound by CPI Group (UK) Ltd, Croydon, CR0 4YY
08/05/2025
01864332-0001